Living
in
Shadow and Light

Roxanne Whatley

Living in Shadow and Light

First paperback edition printed January 2015 USA & Canada
First audio & mp3 editions produced January 2015 USA &
Canada
First digital editions produced January 2015 USA & Canada

ISBN 978-0-9920462-3-1 paperback ISBN 978-0-9920462-5-5
audio cd ISBN 978-0-9920462-4-8 audio mp3
ISBN 978-0-9920462-6-2 kindle/electronic

Published by HarteMedia Worldwide
For more copies of this book, please email:
bookinquiries@HarteMediaWorldwide.com
For speaking, media, or other author inquiries, please email:
lisaljen@thevanadisgroup.com Tel: 17786546548, extension 4
Designed and Set by Vanadis Media www.vanadismedia.com
Printed in Canada and the USA

Contents

Acknowledgements

1

Preface

3

Forward - Before We Begin

17

Living in Shadow and Light

22

I Don't Know Anyone This Has Happened To

33

It's Not That Big A Deal

46

The Four Root Origins

57

She Has A Restraining Order, It's All Good

73

He's In Jail, So She's Okay

85

He'll Never Change

99

Women Like Me

111

We All Have A PoP

147

A Note About Gender

163

What Now?

166

Domestic Violence Solutions

172

About the Author

176

Acknowledgements

I would love to publicly thank -

Nancy Feehan, from off pager to silhouette in the fog that fateful night when my world forever shifted on its axis, I am more grateful to you than I can express. Your seasoned, reasoned, open heart & continuing friendship I treasure.

Richard Nicole, for standing by me as I made some colossally bad judgment calls in the 'trusting people' department, but allowing me (no matter how frustratingly) to learn that my 'who to trust' meter was faulty as part of the problem, and to fix it myself in the ways I find most comfortable. Even when you wholeheartedly disagree with my final decision.

Sandy Cumberland, genuine heroine of your own life, your openness and willingness to shape your own destiny inspired me through the last dredges of disintegration of the wheels that fell off my apple cart years ago. I know that sentiment made no sense to any other than you, and for that I adore you, as well.

Denise Blade, whose prominent 'stand up for yourself & don't take crap from anyone' gene is so strong; sharing with me the words of your Nan which I now carry in my pocket "Love many, trust a few, always paddle your own canoe" - perfection in timing.

And to the women, kids, and men who have opened themselves up to finding their own demons, darkness, pain and fears so they could stop their own cycles of violence, putting it behind them to discover healing and wholeness, embracing living in their shadow and light - I can't find the words to let you know how proud I am of you. How I am exceptionally grateful to you that you let me come along and participate in your healing, your renewal. Each and every one of you inspire me, every single day, and I celebrate you with everything I am...

Preface

Stephanie J. Kilhefner changed everything.

There have been many times, even up to this very second, where I wonder what in the world I'm thinking, writing this book, stepping resoundingly out into the light.

I like being invisible. It suits me.

I have a public face where I am accomplished, successful, in business.   I'm good with teaching, mentoring, sharing my expertise in helping others achieve their goals and life choices, create loving relationships which are realizations of heart dreams.   In helping the rescuers be better at rescuing: those people and organizations who provide safe haven and support for women, children, and our companion animals in crisis.

But the private me is *intensely* private. I rock my inner curmudgeon, and it is not a casual thing. I'm good at it. Really good. I like it that way. It is by both nature and design. I have a whopping fifteen, count 'em, 15, 'friends' on FaceBook, most of whom have never been in the same room with me and know very little about my personal life, and even if we were to find ourselves in the same room I doubt they would recognize me. Come to think, one of those 15 is another FaceBook page of mine, so that would be a grand total of 14.

I have only a text plan on my iPhone, godshonesttruth. Talking on the phone, chit chatting, I find …uncomfortable. Often, I simply don't want to talk, at all, to anyone. I love to chat, to connect, in the same physical time and space with someone, and I genuinely love people. The phone I just don't do, personally. I can't explain it. Those who are close to me simply know I adore them and they can't call me, but I'm a texting wizard. In my best moments I hope this particular quirk is seen as part of my acquired-taste charm, and in my worst moments I do realize it's a bit of a muddlement and frustration to others. I've come to grudgingly accept it, rather than try to change, and that self acceptance only after years of fighting to change, phone-wise. It must be an odd 'shadow effect,' sort of thing.

Up to this moment I can count on the fingers of one hand, perhaps a hand and a half, the number of people who know about the darkness and fantastical events of my life. Even those, perhaps only a couple of trusted beings know of them all. One of those amazing people happens to be dead, so he isn't really talking. If he is, it takes a special kind of listener, so I feel pretty safe on that one.

My reclusiveness by conscious choice is a result of abuse and degradation which dominated my childhood & teen years, with that abuse only increasing as I moved out on my own. It had to, I knew no other way of life, of living, of relationship, of navigating.

As kids, we don't know it's abusive, degrading, destructive, demeaning. It's difficult, we know, but, just 'life,' right?

Moving through relationships which grew increasingly

more denigrating and demeaning, I grew equally more powerless to stop the momentum, try as I might. And, try, I did.

I'm an expert on the dynamics of destructive relationships & domestic violence, the human conditions which contribute to them and sustain them, as well as solutions to interrupt, to prevent, to end cycles of destruction and abuse - because I needed those answers to save my own life.

That is not a lovely figurative catch phrase. I, quite literally, escaped death by the hands of my husband only because of an odd anomaly of my birth which prevented my skull from bursting open as it hit the pavement when I was pushed from our speeding car into oncoming traffic. Through the time following, sliding farther down the rabbit hole, body broken, skull fractured, spirit crushed, pain and concussion trapping my own mind away from my reach at the very time I most needed my wits about me, I visited the depths of hell and powerlessness in scenes I would have sworn were from a classic Dickens-meets-Stephen-King-novel mashup had I not been living them in full blown color.

Along the way, so far, in this life, I've made colossal mistakes in even those small numbers of people I trusted. I've shared painfully vulnerable, emotionally and physically destructive, psychological quagmire, shameful and humiliating and intimate details of portions of my life only to have proven that my trust in the safety of the relationship was sorely misplaced. The kind where, after the stings of betrayal, you crawl back into the dark lonely corners to lick your wounds wanting your final whispered words to the person to be "Excuse me, could I just have my vulnerability back, please?" but knowing that ship not only sailed - it was torpedoed and sunk.

Clearly knowing the human beings you can trust, and those you cannot trust - that inner voice and gut feeling - is out of whack in those of us who were raised in abusive environments. In fact, as I would learn working in my own research as well as counseling other women, we tend to have it completely backwards. Our 'trust meters' are faulty, but we haven't a clue that they are.

I own my shadows because as a woman, a person, a human being, who has gone through that darkness, I find my own safety in the dark. Invisibility is my friend. To be visible is the highest of risk to a woman, to any living being, who has been abused mentally, emotionally and physically.

This past year I had the opportunity to be interviewed on a couple of metropolitan area radio shows in the US, each having large listener base. The producers wanted to know about my work with helping women, and men, overcome their abusive relationships and find healing - the work with which I've devoted my very under the radar time and heart over the last twenty years. These radio shows shared a subject of domestic violence as a generality, then the specifics of a topical event. Both involved, directly and indirectly, football sports heroes. Both were incendiary and caused quite the kerfuffle in social commentary, though quite different in scope and what transpired.

These were heated discussions, rife with knee jerk societal & political reactions, the propensity of media types to turn up the rhetoric for the sake of ratings, and the now rampant nameless faceless twitter-verse chiming in an opinion about a subject the commenter knows virtually nothing about. A bit of substance was able to surface when speaking with the occasional listener call-in. It was important to me to have a valuable discussion about the problem, not simply engage in a media firestorm for ratings-sake. Overall, the experience left me frustrated and with quite a bad taste in my mouth.

Domestic violence is a dangerous issue, and to gloss over it, to use it for boosting ratings, or somehow worse - to grab your 2.53 seconds of social media attention - really cranked my feisty side. I understand the game, as a producer and media insider, but this, domestic violence, *is not a game*. Not by a long-shot.

So I pulled my shadows in around me and withdrew to my very practiced, happily reclusive, seclusion and silence.

However, I can no longer find comfort in my silence. In fact the discomfort is almost overwhelming.

It began to bubble this past October. October is designated "National Domestic Violence Awareness Month" in the US. I tend to believe our 'awarenesses' can slip over into Canada and be a North American issue, if not a global, this planet, issue.

Women, kids, husbands or mates, people, trust, vulnerability, relationships, family. It's a people-thing, not a country-thing. Don't you agree?

Domestic violence is an issue of 'us'. You. Your daughter. Your mother. Your sister, cousin, or niece. Your best friend. The woman who works in your department, delivers your mail, flies your aircraft. Your child's social studies teacher. The woman who manages your financial portfolio, or handles the till at the grocery checkout. Your representative in congress, or parliament.

By the same token, 'us' & 'we' are also the deliverer of the abuse. Your son. Your father. Your brother, cousin, nephew. Your best friend. The guy who works in your department, delivers your mail, flies your aircraft. Your child's social studies teacher. The man who manages your financial portfolio, or handles the till at the grocery checkout. Your representative in congress, or parliament.

It was with great anticipation this last October that I waited to see, to hear, to feel those shifts in our perception and the way we deal with domestic violence and spousal abuse. To soak in the sparks of conversation, of openness, of solution. To see the awareness provide more safety - after all, isn't that what an 'Awareness Month' is supposed to do?

October 1st came, and there was silence. That's okay, I thought, it's the first, and there are several other "National Month" causes fighting for our attention. "Tomorrow, that's it…" I reasoned. "Tomorrow."

Tomorrow came, bringing more silence. As did each subsequent 'tomorrow' throughout October bring a more resounding silence.

It's also breast cancer awareness month, which I thought would be a likely harmony with domestic violence. Each is one of the largest killers of women, one of the most deadly, and one of the most difficult battles (so to speak) we women seek to overcome. Along with heart disease, they are the Top 3 killers of women. As with breast cancer and heart disease, we women often do not overcome domestic violence, and the attack takes our life, robbing our families and children of our love, companionship, relationship.

My heart sank as, I kid you not, "Global Hand-Washing Day" (check it out, October 15) made the mainstream media. The height of ridiculous was the double dip of National Chocolate Week and National Curry Week happening at the same time, the week of October 13 - 19. Now, I love me some chocolate, and some curry. I'm quite the fan of both, and together they are even better.

I know the combo is fabulous because there were recipes for using chocolate and curry displayed in all form of media during their 'awareness week'. Our hands were nice and clean, to boot.

All the while I knew that during this "Awareness Month" in

the US & Canada, alone, 227 women were beaten until they were broken. 78 women could no longer attend their school classes or university because they were being abused by a partner they trusted. 876 women were absent from work due to domestic violence related causes. 13 women were killed. Another 485 were demeaned, belittled and berated until they had no sense of self worth remaining, their souls shattered. 26 parents were without their daughter as they buried her, too young, and without a reason which made sense. 31 children were without their mom, because their dad, or her lover, killed her.

Those kids have to live with that. Forever.

The kids who still had their mom watched as she was beaten, stood in their own panic and fear as she lay bleeding and broken and bruised. Some of these kids had the violence and force directed toward their little bodies, hearts, minds, as well. Some were shifted away from her and into foster care.

Those kids have to live with that.

All in silence. Mariska Hargitay, from the US series "Law & Order: SVU," is doing some amazing work in the field of getting conversation started. Meredith Viera came forward as a public figure willing to shake up the antiquated - yet still outrageously prevalent - socio-economic stereotype of the battered woman.

But it isn't enough. Is it?

That's not okay with me.

One of the other causes I champion is helping abused animals, those pets we love today and throw away tomorrow to starve to death on the streets, be hidden away to be tortured as bait/fight dogs, or be killed in our overburdened shelters. Horses who have served their purpose gently, safely, entertaining our kids at summer camp, only to be sold off for slaughter because we can't see fit to take the time find them appropriate homes. Cash for death is better. Hundreds killed, every day. Hundreds.

The tipping point, for me, that straw for this camel's back, was this Christmas.

This Christmas Eve a woman was killed. She was an ordinary woman with an ordinary life. She had a 'micro-rescue' for the slaughter bound horse, meaning she was simply a caring person who had room for one discarded horse, or perhaps two. A safe place, nourishing food, love and attention, training and support until the unwanted horse finds a new family of humans to love it. The 11th hour salvation from death. She wasn't wealthy. She wasn't famous. She had a normal job where she worked every day. She lived quietly on her small farm near a small town in the rural upper east of the US. She had two young children, toddlers.

Christmas. The time of love, of coming together, of peace

and giving. Wrapping presents and carols and bedtime stories after you put out the cookies and milk for Santa.

Yet, for her, Christmas Eve was met with her husband slicing her throat, bashing in her head with an axe, then carving her up. Her kids were in her home. When he was finished killing their mom, he took them to his parents to celebrate Christmas.

That's not okay with me.

That's *not* okay with me.

The comfort of my silence in my own protected world, my pulling in my shadows around me so I can stay safe and invisible, are not worth another woman being killed by the man who tells her he loves her. The woman who believes him when he says so.

That's not okay with me.

So, this is dedicated to Stephanie J. Kilhefner who lost her life this Christmas Eve, and the hundreds of nameless, faceless women just like her who are killed, beaten, belittled, terrorized, crushed and damaged, every day, by someone they love and trust, but in whom they don't see the danger. Stephanie's two children, and all the kids who will face being a kid whose mom was killed because she trusted, & didn't see the danger in, someone she loved. The other women who were killed this Hanukkah and Christmas and Thanksgiving and Tuesday afternoon and Saturday morning simply because they trusted the man they loved, and didn't see the danger in that man.

Together, we can come to a greater understanding of the 'why'. The better questions, deeper and smarter, to discover better answers and solutions. Until we develop that rich, deep, open curiosity about the 'why' we are doomed to keep repeating these cycles. To instead seek the underlying 'why' - which means we have to stop flailing around in our anger and retribution about the 'what happened' - we need a powerful shift of perception, and an equally powerful dose of eye opening blinder removal about the comfortable lies we tell ourselves which only encourage the destruction to continue.

Lies which are killing, destroying, incapacitating, the women we are, and the women we love. These lies are also keeping the men we love trapped in their own cycle of delivering the abuse.

Together, we can interrupt these patterns, shift the behaviors, stop the madness. We don't have to find a cure for breast cancer or heart disease to stop domestic violence, we just have to have better conversations, take smarter and more aware actions.

It's a ludicrous situation, isn't it, domestic violence?

When, together, we can change it?

It's as dangerous and insidious as any cancer, yet, we need

only to use our beautiful human minds, hearts, intellect and awareness to change the cancer that is domestic violence and family abuse. Together, we can do that.

Together, we can do anything.

For one other woman to face degradation, humiliation, debilitation and damage at the hands of someone she trusts is one woman too many. For her children to witness it is unacceptable. For her to die in front of them is reprehensible. For her kids to be victims of the same abuse, even as collateral damage, unbearable.

It's happening even as you read this. It is happening from a man you know, a man you love, a man you care about. It is happening to a woman you know, a woman you love, a woman you care about.

That's not okay with me.

Please, ask yourself: is it okay with you?

❄ ❄ ❄ ❄ ❄ ❄ ❄ ❄ ❄ ❄

Register your copy of this book purchase at http://livinginshadowandlightbook.com/bkbuyer1 and I will give you, as my gift, a copy of the audio book. Simply send a copy of your receipt by visiting the link above, and instructions to grab your gift copy of the audiobook will be delivered to you.

Or, on your smartphone, to register your receipt and receive your gift audio, scan:

❋❋❋❋❋❋❋❋❋❋❋

To find out more about how you can be a part of the solutions for domestic violence so the women you love and care about are safe, please visit Domestic Violence Solutions Alliance .Org (http://domesticviolencesolutionsalliance.org/lisalp)

Or, on your smartphone, to start the conversation for being part of the solution, scan:

❋❋❋❋❋❋❋❋❋❋❋

To discover how easy it is for you to help save a loving dog, purring cat, or beautiful horse from being tortured and killed, please visit Companion Animal Advocates Alliance .Org

(http://companionanimaladvocatesalliance.org/lisalp)

    Or, on your smartphone visit Companion Animal Advocates Alliance.org by scanning:

Before We Begin

This is an odd place to be, standing in my own safe shadows while deliberately reaching out into the light.

One of the biggest challenges we face as the wonderful human beings we are is that of communication. It's consumed me since childhood, this decidedly unique skill of communication that separates us from other creatures on the planet. How words have such power, create such confusion, contain such potential - for harm, good, upliftment or destruction & all shades in between.

Reading is an acquired skill, not one native to our human animal communication base. With words, letters assembled in black on a white page, to convey meaning, intent, story and value, there are so many opportunities for those words to go awry in delivery or in receiving.

With the black word on the white page, you hear the voice, in this case my voice, in your own. The tone, inflection and meaning are as you would use them in your own day to day world. You get none of my cadence, hesitation, softness or dynamic. You hear none of my rise and fall in inflection and intensity, my feistiness rise or my tenderness settle. You don't have opportunity to see my eyes, my movement, my birthing of the words collecting to convey their meaning.

All of these are important clues in understanding one another. With the black word on the white page, most of these vital clues are missing.

Where I've scattered, throughout, various ways of integrating audio, video, images - snippets and nuggets to experience my story outside of the black word on the page - with sincere invitation to take advantage of these offerings, we are together on this journey with my words, black letters on the white page, strung together for you.

So I'd like to share with you where I am, how I am, my feelings & views in creating these words for you, perhaps helping to integrate my meaning into your partaking. To hear the audio of me sharing this section as I write, please register your book purchase at http://livinginshadowandlight.com/bkbuyer, or on your smartphone text LISAL to 12264551275 and the instructions to access your free audio will be delivered to you. You may also scan the code at the end of this chapter from your smartphone and receive your gift audiobook.

I'm picturing you, the reader, in my mind and sensing you in my heart. As if we were curled up in my library or living room, next to the fire with a cup of tea. Sharing as a friend.

This is an exceptionally vulnerable place for me, stepping out into the light, still clinging to my shadow safety. You will discover, through these pages stories and scenes of life from my own as well as those of others I've worked with through the years, that we who are easily victims of abuse and likely people to be taken advantage of by others share a basic life engagement energy of 'within'.

We pull in. We don't share our hurts or fears easily. We don't like to be out in the spotlight, personally. We don't find it comfortable to talk about our 'in here' - the world we live in with heart and mind and soul. We can't imagine hurting someone, or something, else, and would not do so, even if it means we are hurt in the process. At some point, perhaps several points, we have experienced painful retribution on those rare occasions we did try to stand up for ourselves.

It's part of the completion of the 'we can be taken advantage of' cycle, our preference to be invisible. Unlike the nifty cloak granted to Harry Potter, we have to make ours in day to day life, moment by moment. Often we are too good at this difficult feat, and it isolates us too fully from those we might not need to protect ourselves from, at the same time isolating us with the very ones from which we do need protecting.

So this stepping out, this saying - albeit in black words on a white page, for now - out loud in front of god and everybody what happened through my dark journey and my painful 'in here' of life is so far out of the cliche comfort zone I have no words to explain.

You, though reading my words, are a stranger to me. I don't know who you are, or why you gravitated to this book. Such is the nature of stepping out into the light, everyone can see you, if they choose. You can see me, but I can't see you.

From my perspective I had two choices.

One: step out in all authenticity, transparency and openness, withholding nothing; or,

Two: shade, shape and filter to protect those exceptionally humiliating and vulnerable events, places and moments I hold.

The choice was clear. Either do this fully open and honoring my authenticity, or don't do it at all.

So, as you take in the words, in black on this white page, please find me giving them to you in a manner of trust.

My intent is not to cause harm to one other being. You'll find my rule is I will detail a situation or event, and if it would reflect negatively upon a person who is living, I won't use their name. The event and circumstance is the important focus, not to shame, harm or denigrate another person.

I'm not angry, or bitter, or judgmental. My personality has a sarcastic bent, on the dry ironic side, but also slightly goofy, sometimes. Both do slip in, but, again, not at the expense of someone else.

My hope as I release this to you is that you have your cup of coffee, or tea, curled up by the fire in my living room, and receive it as you would the harrowing tales of a good friend.

❊❊❊❊❊❊❊❊❊❊❊

To receive your gift audiobook, on your smartphone scan:

Living in Shadow and Light

Throughout these years of talking about domestic violence and working to find effective answers/solutions, I find a pattern in four relative 'clumps' of people:

1. Those smack in the middle of the destructive relationship as receiver, deliverer, or kids trapped in the environment;
2. Those who are 'first responders' and crisis caretakers - the officers, counselors, shelter workers, nurses and physicians first on the scene with the aftermath of an explosion;
3. Those who are family, loved ones, co-workers, neighbor and friends of those directly or indirectly involved in the violence;
4. Those who are on the outside of direct experience, direct knowledge, or direct association with the domestic violence cycle

The common factor is, no matter your current involvement - or lack of it - in domestic violence, you likely have some pretty mistaken ideas about how it comes about.

Because it's a subject we don't talk about until it's reached the hospital, the shelter, the newswire, the surveillance video or coroners office - the discussion is always 'after the fact.'

'After the fact' conversation is impacted with opinion, perception and immersion in the feelings of what happened, which severely colors and interrupts any conversation or meaningful curiosity about 'why is this happening.'

We in the middle of the violent relationship, then secondarily those of you who love the people who are in the middle of the violent relationship, aren't talking about it before it gets to the first responders, law enforcement, ambulances, emergency rooms, shelters and courts.

When we in the middle of the violence try to talk about it the aspects of denial, blame, guilt, shame, and a thousand other non-beneficial states are aroused, preventing any kind of help. In fact, discussion with the participants in the middle usually serves to escalate and increase the violence, not diffuse.

Silence is required. The disease of domestic violence is its overbearing silence, its need to be secret.

By not talking about it before there is escalation, before, we in the middle of the violence have either no clue, or muddled clues, about the 'why' it is happening. That doesn't help those of you who love us, nor those responding to the emergency, nor those on the outside wanting to discuss it.

With mistaken, muddled, stunted and fear filled ideas of how it comes about, there is no way to begin to fix the problem, to shift it, to change it, to stop it, or to heal it.

Every now and then I bump up against the type of person who believes they have all the answers. Got it, done deal, listen up. Often, this type of person has not been in the middle of the domestic violence relationship, but is in an 'outside looking in' position from exposure to after-the-fact perspectives. This type of person can be vocal, judgmental, or aggressive about their firmly held choices and decisions around domestic violence.

So before we really begin it's time to ask yourself a good question, for both of our sakes. For the women, kids, men involved in these violent patterns who need our help. Your help, my help.

Are you approaching this subject with an open mind? With some curiosity? With intent to discover information and perspective you might not have been exposed to prior to now?

Or, not?

If you honestly, in your mind and heart of hearts, would put yourself soundly in the above description where you genuinely believe that you have the answers, the insight, and your mind made up decisions held about domestic violence - then this book, and I, are not your cup of tea. To proceed will likely frustrate you, no end. Best stop, now, and carry on as you have been.

For the rest of you with genuine curiosity, questions, openness - together we can accomplish miracles.

To understand these complex relationship issues we <u>must</u> approach them with a curiosity. We need to open our minds to more information, better questions which might give us better answers. We need to feel there is something amiss, or outright missing, in the way we currently think about and deal with domestic violence and relationship abuses. We need to hear new, different, and more powerful words that help us.

We need to see what we've been looking at, listen to what we've been saying about it, get a sense of what we've been feeling about it, what we've been doing about it - and conclude that we haven't been effective.

The solutions we have are not solutions, at all. In fact, most solutions we believe we have are actually making the problem worse. That's not what we want, is it?

Remember the old cliche about the fly continuing to bang its face against the window in an attempt to get out? That fly analogy is described as the definition of insanity, constantly repeating the same action over and over again, yet expecting a different result each time. You can bang your face all you want, but if you don't have better information - or, an open window - you're just going to get a whopper of a headache and a banged up face.

We, as a society, as people, are practicing the insanity of banging our faces against the glass and taking aspirin for our headaches that are domestic violence. And that is if we acknowledge it, at all. It's so much easier to ignore.

It's not your fault that you are off-base in your approach, and it's not your fault you would prefer to ignore the situation. That is what we will address and explore, here. Discover how you can no longer ignore it, but also how you can actually easily help solve it.

We sometimes see the effects of domestic violence. An horrific headline of an after-the-fact event crosses our paths, like the one I mentioned in the preface (and if you skipped the preface, as I often do, please take the time to go back and read it. It's important). Or, leaked video surveillance, allowing us a voyeur peek into the moments of delivery of the violence, captivates our attention for awhile. We hear a story of a co-worker or neighbor, anecdotes of why they are bandaged, bruised, or absent.

Each moves us to feel. Each inspires a reaction in us. Each causes us to think, in our own inner voice, about our opinion of the people, and the event, and what should happen at this point. Each shapes our views about domestic violence.

Each still leaves you, us, parents, friends, siblings, loved ones, on the outside looking in.

Here, in these pages, are the stories of us from the inside. We invite you to come in. Not remain just an observer from afar, peeking through headline, video or anecdote, or witnessing the aftermath, but step inside our heart, our mind, our head and our world as we walk through what it is like.

Only in here, with a broader wisdom and that curiosity, can we discover the roots of the problems, the deep underlying issues at play. Only in here, from the inside, do we discover together how to interrupt the patterns. Only in here, from the inside, do we discover where the open window is, and how to put into place solutions that work, answers that make sense so to interrupt the insanity.

The contributing factors we need to address:

- Your misconceptions and misperceptions about domestic violence
- Our misconceptions and misperceptions about domestic violence
- Silence: we need the silence; you let the silence exist by ignoring - so violence thrives
- Manipulation of the fruit doesn't heal the root, it just makes more rotten fruit - and our collective societal reactions are exclusively manipulating the fruit
- Using force on a weak recipient destroys; inviting, sharing and teaching use of strength elevates the weak into their own strength

Abuse lives behind closed doors - surveillance video aside. If you think about it, even the surveillance video was a 'behind closed doors' situation.

Abuse lives in silence, hidden and secretive. It needs the darkness, the hiding, in order to thrive.

No one in the abusive relationship speaks about it, about what goes on. We can't. Occasionally the deliverer of the violence and abuse speaks about it - but not as violence or abuse. When they speak of it it is because they have self justified the actions they took, the beatings, the verbal dishing out, the harassment and denigration they delivered.

If it is spoken about, it is purely because the person speaking has made their actions okay.

And we on the receiving end certainly don't speak about it. In fact, if we are put in a position of direct challenge, we lie about it to cover it up. No one inside the abusive relationship can let the fulness of it be known. Often, we hide it from ourselves, unable to recognize or acknowledge how bad it really is. We certainly can't let anyone outside the relationship know.

That doesn't make sense, does it?

Why on earth would someone being abused not want to talk about it?

Why wouldn't someone being abused beg for help to stop it?

Why wouldn't someone being abused be honest about what is happening, if asked?

Why would someone being abused actually protect their abuser?

Why wouldn't someone being abused stand up for themselves and put a stop to it?

Why?

If you put yourself in that abusive situation, that is what you would do. Share, run, talk, call the authorities, get help, fight back, that's what you would do. You'd shut up, hold your fists by your side, not pick up the hammer or knife or gun, or you would get out, go for a walk, not abuse. And that's if you even got yourself in that kind of position, in the first place.

Therein lies the strongest aspect of the problem and how we are making it worse.

We humans have only our perceptions, our decisions, our experiences.

You view life, make your choices in life, hear your decisions, feel your experiences, inside your own mind and head. You have crafted, drafted, sifted and put together a world that makes sense to you, sounds good, feels right.

As it should be.

Then, however, we beautiful human beings get askew. You have a tendency to use your life choices as the benchmark for others. Everyone else should fit into the decisions, choices, attitudes which you hold correct.

The problem with that is we are each doing that to everyone else. Conflict has begun.

Your friend (or parent, or boss, or child, or government, or....) believes that you need to use the decisions held as 'true' by them, thankyouverymuch.

You believe that your friend (or parent, or boss, or child, or government or....) should use the decisions you hold as 'true,' thankyouverymuch.

Don't, for one moment, try to make that friend (or parent, or child...) use the decisions that you have made.

And you, for one moment, are not very keen to let go of your choices, decisions and beliefs to instead live those of your friend (or parent, or boss, or....)

Every person holding the same relative belief: "I've got the answers that work - so you take them, because I'm right (and you are not)."

Of course, it isn't as clear and easily understood as that. We don't consciously know that's what we are doing to one another. But that's what we humans do.

In the case of domestic violence, you, in your world, would never harm a child. You would never use fists, hammers, words, knives, guns and other weapons of singular destruction to hurt a woman, a child, an animal...you just...wouldn't. You might think about it in some form during your fits of anger, but actually acting on it, carrying it out, never.

It's inconceivable to you.

For that, I'm grateful.

However, for those involved in the domestic abuse cycles, it is more than conceivable. It's normal.

You, unable to participate in either end of the domestic violence cycle, holding your own 'how and why' as you have decided, cannot help.

You, however, with your clearer, stronger, knowing from outside the cycle, can be of great benefit if you can step inside and factor in what goes on within the cycle.

You live in the light.   You live where domestic violence, battered woman syndrome, and abuse are concepts of a type of reality.

We live in the shadows.   We live where domestic violence, battered woman syndrome, and abuse are our normal life, and our day to day reality.

Two entirely different mindsets. Two entirely different thought processes.   Two entirely different ways of navigating.   Two entirely different decisions. Two entirely different safety zones.

In order for us, as receivers of abuse and violence, to learn to live in the light, we must see, hear, feel and believe more of the way you on the outside believe.

In order for us, as receivers of abuse and violence, to learn to find peace in our shadows, we must see, hear, feel and believe that we are in control of our safety, our body, our world.

You cannot, no matter how you try, force your sense of life choices and views upon us. It's like trying to force purple to be orange, or the Beach Boys to be Usher. We have to take our own steps to integrate your world, your reality, your concept of right/wrong and healthy/unhealthy into ours in ways that make sense to us. We have to do it, ourselves.

You can help, but you can't force. You can support and walk with, but you can't push and do it for us.

We, as receivers of domestic violence, will always have those experiences.   It is up to us to find our 'survivor' so we can replace our 'victim'.

I will always feel uneasy in some situations that won't make sense to you. Often, it makes no logical sense to me, either, but the unease still prevails.

I will always feel a strange vulnerability around others, and that vulnerability will not make sense to you if you have not been abused and treated with violence by someone you trusted.

I will always feel some form of distrust in my own ability *about* trusting someone else, based on my experiences trusting the wrong people and the blowback from those mistakes. I have sort of a blind trust for everyone, as do a lot of women who have been abused since childhood. That serves us poorly, and is part of our dynamic of finding ourselves smack in the middle of a relationship with someone who clearly, obviously, should not have had our trust. That might not make sense to you, our sound right to you, if you have not been abused.

Because of that, I will always need my shadow, to slip into invisibility, to remove myself from view and reach of 'others.' But to be healthy, and to live a full life, I need to be safe and comfortable in the light with the rest of the world.

The delicate balance is to live in shadow and light. To know when I need both. To continue growing about how I can understand when one is appropriate and the other not.

The women I work with who have been victims, and are determined to call themselves survivors, live in the same situation: discover their balance of living in shadow and light.

When you, from your stronger, clearer, inconceivable outside, can understand that about us is the point where you become help, benefit, and part of the solution.

Let's take a look at how we on the receiving end of abuse are handling the situation, the internal factors contributing to the violence & destruction in the first place, and combine that with some of the lies you might be living with that are making the situation worse.

We need you to let go of these lies, and replace them with some truths. We need to recognize our own destructive self-lies, and replace them with some truths. We all need to understand the inner workings of the abusive situation.

Together...

Next Steps:

To listen to audio, watch a video, or sit in - as my guest - on my next web masterclass about how to find out more about how domestic violence is hiding in plain sight in your life, with a woman you love and care about, please visit

- ◆ On the web, go to http://livinginshadowandlight.com/shadow
- ◆ On your smartphone, text SHADOW to 12264551275, and an invitation link will be sent back to you immediately

Shadow and Light Lie #1
"I Don't Know Anyone This Has Happened To"
And
"I Can't Tell Anyone, They Won't Understand"

Maggie* was sitting in the coffee shop waiting for me. I had a general description, but I really didn't need it. Women who are being abused have a different look and feel about them. You probably wouldn't pick up on it, but having been so severely abused for so long, and after the hundreds of other women I've worked with, I can pick it up across a crowded room. She puts my intuition on high alert.

She was in her late 30's, dark blonde hair, and soft blue eyes with mild crinkles on the outer corners. She had an easy smile, strong handshake and gentle presence. Her eyes had a tinge of sadness in them, as if her soul was aching, and there were stories to tell hidden in their depths. Stories, I knew, that had been long secret and she likely wouldn't dream of telling.

Maggie had been married to Jake for about 13 years. She waited to marry until she had established her career in financial planning, and she wanted to make sure she was mature enough, marrying 'the right one'. We laughed when we tried to figure out just what 'mature enough' and 'the right one' might have meant, but mostly she just didn't want to make the same mistakes her parents did: marrying too young, not enough wisdom about life, themselves, money, etc.

She was attracted to Jake initially because of his 'take charge' attitude. Jake was almost fearless, she said. Her inclination was to think, think, and think again, before moving forward, and possibly thinking more before taking action. I knew that was her basic root life pattern, her natural life engagement pattern. Jake was one of the four root life expression types that makes things happen, a very outward 'go-go' movement in life. He was the kind of man who loved the grand gesture - roses, champagne, chocolate and the limo to the 'we're the only ones in our favorite restaurant tonight' - for a simple date night.

Jake had lots of friends, was always busy with parties, networking, sports and work. Maggie had people she knew, but was more comfortable with just a few, close, friends. She didn't like cocktail parties or big tailgate sporting events. She did have fun when a small group went to a good game, but she liked quiet time with her own thoughts. Something, at first, that Jake complimented.

This afternoon Maggie was dressed nicely, wearing a cashmere sweater the color of cloves so gorgeous I didn't hesitate too long when I told her I'd be okay with it if she decided she hated the sweater and gave it to me, instead. She was casual expensive, good taste. I actually thought when I saw her that it would be something Ivanka Trump would wear. Maggie was CEO of her own firm, handling the financial portfolio's of some pretty impressive small business and Fortune 1,000 companies. From being a high level banker, myself, in another life way back when in my late twenties, I know that's not easy. Her field is highly, highly, back bitingly competitive. You also have to be good at what you do. Really good. Quadruply good as a woman in a still-boys-world of money.

I offered to get her a refill on her coffee so she didn't have to try to stand with the cast on her leg. Though her very on-trend wide leg pants covered it pretty well, and she did a good job hiding it discretely under the table, it extended from her toes to just over her knee. I didn't know what injuries she had before I showed up and I didn't ask after I arrived because when you are talking with someone who received their injuries from the hand of their mate, you don't ask. You create an environment where they can share what they choose, and that's important.

After about fifteen minutes of small talk around the general economy and some of the characters we had both encountered in the financial world, Maggie began to relax a bit. Her pretty blue eyes dimmed, and then filled with tears. Often, women won't really share what is going on until we meet half a dozen times, sometimes more. Establishing trust with others to talk about what happens to us in our abusive relationship is not our strong suit, and I respect that so much because knowing who (and who not) to trust is my particular bugaboo. I've gotten that one woefully wrong more often than right over most of my life, so I understand the caution. Meeting as often as it takes - that's okay. Today, though, Maggie was ready to talk, so I became quiet.

Maggie had not told one single soul, ever, of the abuse in her relationship with Jake. I was the first. One of the nurses in the emergency room had slipped her my contact information after Maggie's injuries were treated. I know a lot of women receive the same quiet slipping of paper, with only soft eye contact and "here is someone who understands and can help..." the only words spoken. I know most women don't contact me, and it breaks my heart. From being in the same situation, I understand. I couldn't, wouldn't, talk with anyone, either.

Also, a familiar, yet disturbing pattern: Maggie had received my contact information not for her latest visit to the emergency room, but for a visit three or four prior. This time, for Maggie's own reasons, was the time she chose to act on it.

Jake began by making denigrating comments, just slight digs

at her, about her. Her looks, her ability to be a good wife, about how she wasn't like the other wives who were outgoing. After a few months, he moved into questioning where she went, why it took so long at the grocers, and who she had lunch with, insinuation and accusations following. After a few years, he began to put down her friends, become upset if she spent too much time with them. She had slowly cut herself off from most of her already small outside world engagement. She met clients at the office, or as part of a team if out at a restaurant for lunch, never after work, no longer in the evening.

The first night Jake slapped her it took her by surprise. The emotional sting was more than the pain on her cheek. She was stunned, and froze. She began to cry softly, and Jakes response to her tears was to punch her in the eye with is fist. She crumbled, hid her face, and curled into the fetal position in her chair. She was trying to hide herself, partly so he would stop, partly because she was in shock, confused, ashamed and embarrassed. He did stop, storming out of the house. They spent the next week in silence before Jake began to act as if it had never happened. Maggie thought perhaps it was a one time thing, she needed to pretend it didn't happen. She was afraid to bring it up, afraid it would possibly trigger more of the same. She wasn't sure what she would even say, anyway. Silence was best, she decided.

The verbal violence increased, first. She didn't know what to do, or what Jake was going to do, so she would sit, eyes averted, until he stopped. She didn't want to provoke him, nor make it worse in any way. When after a few months of non-stop verbal abuse she decided to leave the room when Jake started, he began combining the physical violence with the verbal assaults.

She didn't tell anyone. Who would she tell? What would she say? Jake was a good man, a good husband, a respected businessman. She wasn't really sure what was happening, or why it was happening, but she knew she could figure it out. Figure out how to stop him, to turn back the time so they could be good together, again. Most of the time, even through this turmoil, they were still good together. They made a good team, and cared deeply for one another.

She feared her reputation in the financial field would crumble if word of this got out. People, clients, would no longer see an accomplished, seasoned and respected financial player. Instead, they would see a woman who is weak, who is out of control of her personal life. They would see her as a victim, and you don't want a victim of anything managing your financial portfolio. More, she would see herself as a victim, and in her own mind, she was not. This was a situation that she could find a solution to, if she just held on, kept trying, and kept quiet.

Friends would ask what was going on. Her dad even mentioned something. Maggie was mortified. Her dad? Her own shame leapt to the forefront and she flatly denied anything was wrong. There was no way she could tell her dad what was happening. Not only would he not understand, he would pop into his 'godfather mode' and Jake would simply be vanquished with a car ride to the desert one night never to be seen nor heard from again. Her dad would also, forever, have that look in his eyes whenever he saw Maggie, of his little girl, as victim. She didn't want that and couldn't live with even the thought.

After a few years the violence had established a pattern. Jake no longer left bruises or broke skin where they could be seen so she could still go to work, secret undiscovered. He never broke another limb after her first broken arm because it was difficult to explain. She drove to different emergency rooms in different hospitals so no one would see the pattern.

Until that night. That night, she had reached her own, quiet, internal limit. He had broken her ribs, she knew. He had done it before, so she could tell.   He was getting more directly threatening, verbally, instead of just demeaning and put downs. The frequency and intensity of his outbursts were increasing. She was feeling scared more and more, effecting her work, for the first time.   She wasn't rebounding and healing as quickly, and found herself more susceptible to colds and flu's going around.

That night, after she was sure he was asleep, she snuck out to the garage to slip away. She had left a bag packed at the office and secretly arranged to take a week off of work. That way she could be alone with her thoughts, figure out what to do.   All she needed to do was slip away, this night.

She looked in the rear view mirror as she began backing out of the garage and into the driveway, only to see the garage door closing behind her.   The darkness enveloped her with the closing of the garage door at the same time Jake used his spare key to unlock the drivers door and pull her out by her hair. He hit the already broken ribs, and then started on the other side of her back. The darkness seemed to give him more confidence and rage.   He stood on her shin and jumped as the bone cracked in two places. The pain knocked her unconscious.

Maggie remembered his words: "How dare you try to leave me, you stupid bitch.   I thought you were smarter than that, but I guess not. If you ever try to leave me again, I'll kill you. Even if I have to hunt you down, I'll kill you. If anyone finds out about this, I'll kill you."

When she came to, it was light out. Jakes car was gone. He had left her laying there, broken, unconscious, on the cold concrete garage floor as he left for work in the morning. She fell out of consciousness, again, before she was lucid enough that afternoon to call an ambulance. It was nightfall, almost 24 hours later, before she was seen by doctors.

Talking with Maggie, she had the same misunderstanding and misperception that you, who have not been through this kind of thing, have. In hearing Maggie's story, she fit into one of the 'classic 7' with domestic violence misperceptions. Of the 7, hers was

Shadow and Light Violence Pattern #1:

Maggie thought:

- I can't tell anyone;
- If I do tell anyone, they won't understand, I'll be humiliated and lose everything;
- If I do tell anyone, he will kill me;
- No one else is going through this;
- He's a good man, so maybe I am doing something to cause this;
- He does love me, and I love him, so we can figure this out - I can;
- He's a good man in almost every way, and I wouldn't want to hurt him by letting anyone know about this - we can stop it ourselves

You think:

- If it was someone I know and love, she would tell me;
- Of course she would feel telling me, or someone, is the right thing to do;
- I would understand if my sister, my cousin, my mother, my best friend financial planner confided in me about

this;

- The guy needs to be caught, and then he'll stop, because he knows better;
- Since no woman I love is talking with me about this, it obviously isn't happening to any woman I know and love

Understanding, seeing clearly, why Maggie would have felt she couldn't tell anyone helps all of the Maggie's I've worked with, and those of you women reading this who are recognizing you are Maggie.

It also helps you, those of you who know and love a Maggie, begin the process of unraveling this set of dangerous lies.

The Living in Shadow and Light Truths we need to hold are:

For the Maggie's:

- You can tell someone, definitely not everyone, or many people, but you can tell one someone who can help, set your firm parameters of what you need from that person, specifically, and exactly - with their firm commitment to provide it for you; you need to share this with another head and mind outside of your own;
- You can find someone who will understand, not lots of people, maybe not many people, but there is someone who understands and can provide good guidance for you that won't make things worse
- If you are in the situation so close to the edge that he would follow through on that threat, don't deny it. You can make a good plan that will have you safely out of harms way before he discovers, and keep you safely out of harms way (you need both!)
- Yes, other women are going through it as you read this;

and other women have made it out safely and stayed safe. There is hope, there is a way ideal for you, and you are not alone in your experience

- He might be a good man in many ways, and he might genuinely love you. The problem is not the good man, or the love. The problem is that he thinks it's okay to treat you this way, and is going to continue. Love has nothing to do with it, and we women want to mix those two. "If he loved me, he would stop" - or "He does love me, so he will stop". This has nothing whatsoever to do with love. It has to do with expressing anger, frustration, and entitlement to hurt you. You must find how to separate those two.

- This one situation is virtually impossible to 'figure out' or solve between the two of you. There needs to be an ability to see the 'why' it is happening, the beginnings of the thoughts or emotions - what happens before Jake gets to the point of violence? What happens to you, inside you, after, so that the cycle continues? You need better questions, and tools to look in different places, different thoughts, different feelings, different aspects of each of you, separately. That is very difficult to do from within the problem - no matter what the problem is. In domestic violence, it's even more difficult to do by yourself.

For those of you with women you care about:

- There is a woman you know, care for, and love, going through this - so you can learn how to be someone she can confide in

- There is a woman you know, care for, and love, going through this - and you can help her discover what she needs to feel safe, find her way out; at the same time stay in control of your own emotions and agenda enough that you don't make things worse and she doesn't get hurt in the process

- ◆ This is not about 'catching the guy so he will stop' - it's about getting her safe and keeping her safe. That is a huge, important, vital mind shift. It's about her, not about him. Believe her, and default to the attitude that if she opens up or seeks help he will follow through on a threat to harm or kill her. Don't take that lightly

- ◆ One in four women is experiencing some form of domestic violence and abuse, in North America. Possibly more, because it is under reported - we don't tell anyone! One of those women is someone close to you, your sister, your cousin, your daughter, your mother, your friend. Do not assume that because no one has said anything that means it isn't happening!

*Maggie is not her real name; Jake is not his. She has worked herself into a healthy place with her shadow and light, and I won't stir up problems by using any identifiers for she and Jake. Each agreed to let me tell their story on condition each would not have to revisit that story, and it could not be ferreted out and assigned to either of them, today. I heartily, and completely, agreed.

The point of sharing their story is to illustrate and relate how their dynamic played out, once discovered. How we were able to see their strengths, their not-so-strongs, and how each was an individual unbalanced. When we were able to see how the separate imbalances played out, then we could see how the mutual dynamics between them were so destructive. These were two people who really did love each other, but did not have a clue about themselves nor one another in life engagement patterns.

You cannot fix what you don't know is broken, and you can't solve what you are not seeking solution for. You can't find solutions in the same mix as the problems, you need outside, new, fresh, and different ideas, concepts, tools and strategies. Once they saw what was broken, and sought workable solutions, each was able to solve their individual imbalance and find a peace with one another and the relationship. Each took the time and attention to healing the deep imbalances carried within, separately.

They did not stay together, but their parting is understood and accepted by each of them. Maggie does not need to fear turning a corner somewhere, or answering the door one night, and Jake following through on his threats to kill her or harm her. Jake worked hard to remove the basis of the threat by understanding his own behavior causing his anger and outbursts. Jake hasn't had a violent or aggressive reaction to any event in the three years since he completed his domestic violence aversion and root behavior training.

We can explore how we reached this healthier point, for both of them.

Shadow and Light Better Questions #1

"If it is so hard for her to let anyone see, or know about this, what woman in my life that I care about is having to hide?"

"If I could find someone who would understand, how could I do that, what would that look like, and what should I do?"

Let's understand the basic dynamics that are in play in this relationship.

For the moment, we need to let go of what is happening, the actions and reactions. When we know it is someone we love, or it is happening to us, the event moves out of our head and into our heart.

When we are at a safe distance, and it isn't personal, any reaction or engagement is largely intellectual, even if we have emotional reactions such as anger, revenge, and such. It's the same system of reaction, no matter the subject. If we aren't directly involved, it's in our imagination, our thinking, our ponder, our observe from a distance.

When it hits home, and we are confronted with it in our very personal and intimate lives, the event and circumstance drops down into experience we own, not just think about. We are more immersed, emotions are higher, more present, no matter what those emotions are.

So our Maggie, who is your sister, daughter, mom or friend, is married to Jake. Jake might be your brother, your son, your dad or your friend. Let's start there.

Next Steps:
To listen to audio, watch a video, or sit in - as my guest - on

my next web masterclass about how to find out about the root tendencies and behaviors for Maggie types and Jake types, for you or someone you love,

- On the web, go to http://fourrootorigins.com/maggie
- On your smartphone, text MAGGIE to 12264551275, and an invitation link will be sent back to you immediately
- Or, you can simply scan the code on your smartphone:

Shadow and Light Lie #2
"It's Not That Big A Deal"
And
"It Isn't That Bad, I Can Handle It"

SuzieQ met me after her dance class one rainy evening. It was one of those icky cold nights, the wet not bad enough to keep your windshield wipers busy, but was bad enough that without them you were driving in a wet haze. The kind of cold that sinks into your bones. Just the night you want to stay curled up toasty warm in with bad SyFy reruns rather than go out anywhere.

What got me out, rather than reschedule, is the message Suzy left on my voicemail. She was upbeat and perky. Her name, of course, is not SuzyQ. I chose that pseudonym for her because it suits her, and is pretty darn close to her real name. Suzy had a lilt in her voice, and an easy laugh that was almost spontaneous giggle. Now, Suzy was calling me because the woman who runs her local women's shelter had given Suzy my contact details. Most callers who are not high or drunk do not giggle when calling me about domestic violence. Just … doesn't…happen. Suzy wasn't high, and she wasn't drunk.

Her voice was tinged with anxiety as she gave me some brief details. Her boyfriend had been getting increasingly more violent with her. His brand of violence was icy cold, rather than explosive. He would get very close to her, press his body up against hers, smashing her against the wall as he verbally dissected her. Cruel, viscous, demeaning words, delivered with cool precision and cunning. The more he could see she was hurting, the more he seemed to enjoy it, and it spurred him on.

Paul, I call him, had taken to grabbing her upper arms in his grip and squeezing until her hands went numb from lack of circulation. There were two fingers on her left hand that still had not 'woken up' from his last bout.

As she detailed for me on her message, the words she chose to end with sent chills through me. "Well, really, I guess it's okay. It's not that big a deal. He doesn't *really* hurt me, or anything."

I tracked her down, bundled up for the nasty night, and out I went.

SuzyQ is happy. She would describe herself as happy, and for the most part, I would agree. She is one of the four root origin types that naturally expresses outward. Her type is outward and up. Everything is good, the cup is more than half full, and there is some measure of natural innocence and fun to be had everywhere.

Paul was a computer programmer. Excellent at numbers, sort of a savant. He had the cool good looks to go with his cool demeanor. Paul didn't laugh much, and his sense of humor was more literal. He didn't really get metaphor, or other kinds of jokes, although he did love good slapstick humor. He was pretty methodical, and what armchair mental health 'experts' after watching too many pharmaceutical commercials might call "OCD". He needed his world 'just so.'

As SuzyQ repeated to me while the kettle was on for tea in the back of her dance studio, he's a good guy. He cares for her, very much. He's an ideal boyfriend, other than the pressing against the wall with viscously cruel words and arm numbing thing. He picks up after himself. Is a great cook, even does the grocery shopping. He enjoys her company, most of the time. He remembers her birthday, their anniversaries, her sisters graduation day. He brings her little tokens, just because.

Suzy was flitting from one task to the next, light on her feet, like the dancer she is. Everything about Suzy was upward and light. The way she held the kettle to pour the hot water into our mugs. Picking up the spoons to put on the table. Gesturing with her hands moving upward as she spoke. That youthful look and the sound in her voice.

I asked if people ever thought she was a child when she answered the phone. Her look of surprise was priceless. "Yes! How did you know that!" she responded with her now trademark kind of giggle. If I had to guess, without knowing, I would have pegged her about 20. 22, tops. SuzyQ was 42 years old. She wasn't childish, or childlike. She was smart, accomplished and quick. She was exceptionally bright. She had started her studio when she dropped out of high school at 17. They wanted to drug her, too. Only with Suzy, everyone thought she had ADHD because she couldn't sit still, needed to be up, moving. Her mind was moving so fast. Her body needed movement. She was not the type of student who could sit still in a seat and focus upon concept or words on a page.

To the outside observer she seemed scattered and flighty. She was called airhead. She was teased that she never settled down, was always hyper, and could be easily distracted by the next shiny object. So many thoughts moved through Suzy's mind, it was hard to keep up. It was hard for anyone other than Suzy to keep up, though. To her, each thought & idea was thoroughly interesting and captivating.

She was attracted to Paul for his ability to be still, and silent; but also his appreciation of her speed, and activity. When I asked what seemed to set Paul into one of his icy compression phases toward her, she honestly couldn't tell. It didn't seem to have a rhyme or reason, it just 'was, in an instant.'

She thought if she could predict it better she could just get out of the way, and all would be well. Because, after all, it really wasn't that big a deal. She had seen tv shows, and was well read about what happens in a "real" domestic violence situation. "We all watch the news," she explained to me, "and Paul is never like any of the domestic violence you see there. Paul isn't violent, he's just..."

Her words trailed off as she fought to find the right phrase for what Paul was doing. She surprised herself when she couldn't really dismiss it as easily as she had been.

I asked to see her fingers, and she gladly shared. Her arms were covered and she looked me in the eye when she asked if I wanted to see her 'colors.' That's how she referred to her bruising, because it was easier for her to live with if they were colors rather than results of violence at the hands of the man she loved. The man she knew loved her.

Her colors were vivid. Black, green, reds and purples. Her fingers were swollen, larger and thicker, than the rest of her small hand. They were very, very cold. I asked if she had seen any kind of doctor, at all. She said she was afraid to, because if she explained how it happened, that the doctor would have to report Paul, and she didn't want that.

Because it wasn't that big a deal. They will heal. Or it isn't that bad if they don't.

Talking with Suzy we needed to determine why it was okay for someone - anyone - to do that to her.

How, in her life and world, did she arrive at a point where it was okay for someone to press her against a wall and say cruel demeaning vicious things to her, about her, at her? How, in her life, did she arrive at a place where it was okay for someone to grab her so hard and so long that for the days following she could barely lift her arms due to the bruising, and to the extent that two fingers will likely be paralyzed for the rest of her life?

What happened in SuzyQ's history that resulted in her even remotely believing that this kind of treatment was okay?

Because Suzy is one of the outward root expressions and her expression of life tends upward, she isn't easily moved down. Whereas Jake, from our last marriage, was the full on forward thrust outward, Suzy was the light, upward, fresh and youthful type of upward. She simply did not retain bad or negative things, situations, events. They would have been like trying to hold down a cork in water. The moment it is released, it pops right back to the top and to attempt keeping it down is a struggle.

When digging through her past, a decidedly 'we need to sit down and investigate' energy which is so opposite to her bubbly up, it was a challenge for me to make it a game. I'm more the "inward, detail, please don't see me/don't worry about me/are you okay?" type of expression. When I explained her energy, her natural way of engaging life, I could see some of her ideas and mind activity line up.

She began to help me decipher and filter through, curious about how I was so different from the way she is in thinking, in using our minds. How were she and I so different in the way I'm comfortable in life? I loved her curiosity.

Together we discovered how the very thing that makes SuzyQ 'SuzyQ' - that bubbly, upward, lilting sweet energy swirl, is the one thing both of her parents and all three siblings found more irritating than a swarm of mosquito's on a hot summer night. Those are not my words, but the words her parents gave to her when she was about 6. They would tie her waist to her seat to make her stay at the table, not talk so much. They would tie her into her bed so she wouldn't get up and roam around the house early in the morning. They would tie her to her chair until she finished all of her homework, alone, even if it took hours. They admonished her to shut up, keep quiet, stop yammering, that her chatter was the worst nuisance and only showed to prove how scatterbrained she was.

And the stories went on, and on, and on, about restraining her physically to try to restrain her active little mind. SuzieQ is like a handful of helium balloons you are asking to be boat anchors. To say it's impossible is an understatement.

She believed that these actions were because they loved her, and wanted the best for her. She believed that there was something wrong with her mind, and something wrong for her to always be happy, see the best in things. She learned that she would never amount to anything because she was so internally active. She couldn't even actually sit in the audience through one of her own dance productions.

SuzyQ had learned that people who love you will point out how different you are and how unacceptable you are, and try to force you to be 'better.' SuzyQ, sweet, gentle, pretty and brilliant bundle of energy SuzyQ, had learned that everything that makes her unique was wrong. And it was okay to tie her up, silence her, isolate her and force her to change.

It was all I could do not to cry as she related one horrific experience after the other. Part of it was the vision of someone tying a little towhead girl to her chair to make her be still and quiet; part of it was the way she felt tinges of hurt but so easily moved back up into dismissing it all as no big deal. My heart ached for this little girl whose magic was so unseen by those around her, so much so that they tried everything they could to destroy it. Now, this woman before me who so naturally made it 'okay' and 'no big deal' for the man she loved to squeeze her until her fingers were paralyzed.

Paul did love her, she was right. She loved him. First we needed to dig through her feelings and beliefs about what love was, how love acted, and how she engaged in those self held beliefs. Second we needed to delve into Paul's natural root energy type, to find out where he believed it was okay to be so verbally vile to anyone, much less a woman he loved. When did Paul get the notion that using his hands to destroy flesh, veins, tissue and fingers was even remotely acceptable?

Talking with Suzy, she had the same misunderstanding and misperception that you, who have not been through this kind of thing, have. In hearing SuzyQ's story, she fit into a different one of the 'classic 7' with domestic violence misperceptions. Of the 7, hers was

Shadow and Light Violence Pattern #2:

Suzy thought:

- He didn't *really* hurt me, not like he could have;
- If I can just see it coming, I can get out of the way and it won't happen;
- Since he didn't hurt me, and it heals, it's not that big a deal;
- Since it's not that bad, it will get better, and he'll stop
- I'm difficult to live with and be around because I'm so flighty and airhead, so Paul is actually patient as a saint with me
- I talk too much and too fast, and that has always been a problem for my family, so sometimes Paul just gets too stressed out about me, I understand

You think:

- If she doesn't think he really hurt her, I should believe her;
- She's smart, and she can figure it out, if it is happening and bothers her enough;
- Maybe it really isn't that big a deal, we all get a little out of hand, now and then;
- He probably will stop, it isn't that bad, so it will fix itself;
- Maybe she is annoying, but he still doesn't have the right to do that to her;
- That isn't love, and he could not possibly love her if he was abusive and violent to her, she needs to wise up about this guy
- Since no woman I love is talking with me about this, it obviously isn't happening to any woman I know and love (yes, my sweet, this is a recurring theme…it belongs here, too)

Understanding, seeing clearly, why SuzyQ would have come to the conclusion that it's not that bad, and it will go away, helps Suzy to interrupt the pattern and make sure it stops. To take her own power, in her own way, to end the abuse. It helps you Suzy's to see yourself in her story, and do what you need to do for your own relationship and health.

It also helps you, those of you who know and love a SuzyQ, begin the process of unraveling this set of dangerous lies.

The Living in Shadow and Light Truths we need to hold are:

For the Suzy's:

- Hurting someone doesn't have degrees, there is a very clear difference between love & respect, and causing harm...it is never, ever, okay to hurt someone 'just a little bit';

- You might very well be able to see it coming, but the point is it shouldn't be there for you to have to avoid in the first place;

- Just because you are understanding about the emotional and physical pain, and there is no scarring visible (let's forget about numb fingers, for the moment), does not mean that someone didn't intentionally inflict hurt and pain at you, on you, to you;

- Yes, he loves you, and yes you love him, but that has nothing to do with how he handles his anger, frustration, and moods. It isn't up to you to apologize or understand his negative behavior, it's up to you to understand why you think it's okay for someone to treat you badly - particularly someone you love and who loves you

- Oh, my, it **_IS_** that bad...that it *is*, at all, is bad; it's not okay, ever, to any degree, at any time, period! Oh, my...

For those of you with women you care about:

- There is a woman you know, care for, and love, going through this - and if she is out of balance enough that she honestly believes this is okay, then that is cause for alarm for both of you

- There is a woman you know, care for, and love, going through this - and she is probably brilliant lightning fast smart, no doubt, but she has a big warning sign flashing saying that she has this little area way out of whack so is likely not in a place to figure out how to stop, avert or end - particularly if she is downplaying the abuse

- This is not about the guy coming to his senses because it 'isn't that bad so he can just stop' if you give him enough time; unless new information is discovered - by the guy - that information giving him a clue that his behavior is not okay so he might want to figure out how to stop, then it isn't going to stop because he doesn't see anything wrong enough in himself

- One in four women is experiencing some form of domestic violence and abuse, in North America. Possibly more, because it is under reported - we don't tell anyone! One of those women is someone close to you, your sister, your cousin, your daughter, your mother, your friend. Do not assume that because no one has said anything that means it isn't happening! (Repeated, in its entirety, from our first case, because it is a significant factor in every case)

We can explore how we reached a healthier point, for both of them.

Shadow and Light Better Questions #2

"If this is happening all around me, even close to me, to a woman I care about, then it is a big deal, so what do I do about that?"

"If I admit that this hurts, and it is a big deal, then I don't want to feel that way, and it isn't okay - what should I do?"

Next Steps:

To listen to audio, watch a video, or sit in - as my guest - on my next web masterclass about how to find out about the root tendencies and behaviors for SuzyQ types and Paul types, for you or someone you love,

- On the web, go to http://fourrootorigins.com/suzyq

- On your smartphone, text SUZY to 12264551275, and an invitation link will be sent back to you immediately
- Or, simply scan the code below from your smartphone:

Rest Stop
Discover the Secret of the
Four Root Origins

There are four basic, what I call 'root origin,' types of people. This work has developed from the beginnings of psychology through to encapsulate the most beneficial of modern mind/brain/body research as well as anthropology and biology models. Combining the best, most powerful, and most effective aspects of each, we come up with a full, holistic, whole being model of who and what we are as human beings. We discover the beginnings, the roots, of our behavior, tendencies and actions.

To be brief, a 'Root Origin' comes before what we learn. We have a widely accepted non-thinking belief that babies are born as these little empty buckets and blank slates. Then, it's up to us as parents, teachers, family & society to 'learn them.'

Learning them is different than teaching them. We need to teach them - to eat with silverware, to tie their shoes and understand the signals to find a bathroom. Learning them is about our expectations and experiences, our choices and attitudes, our hopes, fears, dreams and the gamut of emotions.

So we set about learning them what we expect and intend them to be, to do, and to want. Learn them what we don't want, what they should and should not want, what they should and should not think, what they should and should not feel, and how to mold themselves into behaviors acceptable to all of the expectations around them. We learn them how to hate, what we prefer they like and don't like. We learn them directly, by our intent.

What they learn, however, is usually by observation, listening and feeling the world around them. Think about your own young childhood. You were a brilliant little thing, soaking in actions, tone, movement, result, from everything and everyone around you. What they said to you had a much smaller impact than what you discovered on your own by watching, listening and sensing them. Remember?

When I'm working with those of you in my 'four root origins' trainings & classes, one of my favorite things is when we look in to your own childhood. We take this entirely different perspective and revisit to discover your 'empty bucket and clean slate' stuff others put upon you. The sense of discovery, clarity, and feeling of freedom is palpable. Those moments of discovery of who you really are, under all of those bucket filling and slate written things, is a huge step.

When we really examine, we discover that babies pop out of the womb with some basic tendencies built-in. Factory installed equipment. Base operating systems in their little computers. Definite preferences about the way they engage in their own life. To the extent we recognize those base root already-present tendencies and where they originate, we help the child to understand their strengths and learn to navigate the world by those strengths. These tendencies never leave us, as human beings. These tendencies form our 'roots', as a living, breathing, human animal. We can struggle against them, or we can embrace and develop them.

Primarily we have been taught to struggle against our own root origins and base tendencies. We don't know that we are struggling against, and others don't know they've asked us to struggle against. No one teaches us this stuff, until now, so our parents didn't know. Their parents and grandparents didn't know. None of us knew.

When we do get it, and see this power, it sounds so right. It's quite the opposite of needing to shape the child to our societal and family beliefs. Instead, we look at the child and help he or she become the best they can be with their given, natural tendencies, and blend our loving expectations into Who The Child Really Is but, child first, not us first.

The Four Origins - Maggie and Jake

Two root engagement types go outward in expression; two are inward.

Each is different in their movement and action, whether in, or outward. Each has their own particular strengths, and their own unique challenges.

Each is necessary to the whole of who we are as humans. Somewhere in the last 100 years, or so, we contrived an odd idea that there was a general 'norm' that every human should strive for. A norm in behavior; learning; activity; shape and size; a norm in intellect and how it is measured.

Instead, each basic type has its own 'norm' and power. Together, when we combine our individual norm and power, we realize the idealistic 'sum of our parts is more than the whole' and make it simply realistic. When we combine knowing and known strengths, we automatically balance out the not-so-strongs. We understand and accept the strengths and aptitudes of the others, and we do it with awareness. We are no longer threatened when someone else has a strength that we don't, and we are no longer insecure in ourselves so we don't need to skewer others for the areas that are not-so-strong in them.

Maggie is one of the natural root engagement types that goes inward. Jake is one of the natural root engagement types that moves outward. In fact, Maggie is a 'pull inward and downward' type, and Jake is a 'push outward in a vertical wall' type.

In harmony, these natural engagement types balance one another. Not psycho-babble and co-dependency, but balance.

Maggies pull inward strength combines her comfort with detail, with a slower, fuller and broader movement. It's exactly what makes her a great financial analyst, her ability to chew on details, try on scenario, experiment with ideas and take the 'what if' out to infinity and back. She prefers to be alone in her thoughts, solitary and quiet on the outside. The activity, for

Maggie's, is on the inside. It's reasoned, and complex. If you want a good, solid, all-bases-covered plan, let a Maggie prepare it for you. But, give her time, because her engagement is quieter, and to the outside world of other engagement types, she seems as if she moves slowly. That is by comparison, however….to Maggie, she is moving at Maggie pace, which is just fine to Maggie.

If Maggie were an energy we could see, we would see soft, rolling waves moving in. Sometimes forcefully, like a storm surge, but always in. Waves don't move out, they come in. They move inward, downward, on the horizon. She would sound like a baroque cello. Soft, sensual, low and rhythmic, slow movement. She would feel like a warm afternoon on the porch. She is introspection, pondering, thought and detail.

Jake is the push outward type like the force of nature. He is boisterous, he is go go go. He is 'let's get this thing done' and the follow through. Jake is not the detail guy. He's bright, he's intelligent, he's quick witted and he's activity, itself. If you want a job done, hand it to Jake, and stand back. Done, no lolly-gagging, no messing around, no wishy washy. Jake is hotter, faster, and leads with the end goal in mind.

Jake is full, and a force to be reckoned with, particularly compared to Maggie. To others, Jake seems hot, fiery, and intimidating. Sometimes he can seem the stereotypical testosterone fed male image. It's an unfortunate stereotype, but some aspects are similar in Jake. Action. Activity. Movement outward. Deals. Meet and greets. Party, conversation, lots of to do list items, the more the better. Determination to follow through.

Maggie, in balance, has her not-so-strong with engaging the outside world. She is a nurturer by nature, so putting herself first, or close up there in the mix, is not natural to her. It's a foreign concept. It's what makes her so good at the last detail for caring about her clients.

Maggie, out of balance, pulls in so far on a personal basis that she is incapable and unable to figure herself into the mix. Those details, when scared, when confused, there are even more aspects and versions to consider, think through. This means pulling deeper within, increasing the activity in more to ponder, at the same time her energy slows, bogs down. She is likely prone to depression, as depression, by its very nature is an inward and downward pulling physical and psychological energy. Depression is a weight pulling in and down, making it more difficult to think things through, making it more difficult to engage, hear, see, outward.

Maggie, being an inward, nurturing, put others first engagement type, when out of balance is closer to powerless. Personal power comes with being able to keep yourself healthy, safe, and out of danger. With Maggie's, that means non confrontational, non aggressive, and non threatening reactions. Maggie doesn't go 'outward'. To stand up, push out, fight, is opposite of her comfort, her strength and her ability. When unbalanced, and even deeper back, Maggie cannot suddenly move powerfully in a contrary direction from her very being, and her levels of acceptance.

Maggies cannot hurt another, as hurting another is an outward movement. Maggies hurt themselves, either by accepting hurt, by allowing others to hurt them, or by inaction. Maggies also turn any kind of movement for hurt on themselves, and will hurt themselves, intentionally, such as cutting, food addictions, chemical addictions, and suicide. Of course, there are exceptions to every base personality type, but by and large, Maggies are exclusively inward expressing. Maggies are almost 100% exclusively on the receiving end of violence and abuse.

Jake, when out of balance, releases outward. When someone is angry, and expressing that anger in any way against another, it is a specific movement in their imbalance. It doesn't matter if that anger is in verbal attack, snaking behind anthers back to slander them, picking a fight at a bar or on the street, or harming those more vulnerable than you are such as a woman, child or animal, it's still anger energy releasing.

If we take out the actions, and look at the impetus, we find the place we need to interrupt the pattern. When we are happy, contented, well balanced, or even just frustrated, we don't harm ourselves or anyone/anything else. It's not the energy we have active. Frustration might see a good door slam, or elevated voice shouting match, but the energy and emotion of frustration just doesn't have the whollup and might it needs to be really destructive.

Anger is a response to some form of powerlessness. It doesn't matter if the powerlessness is genuine, or if it's as imaginary as the monster in the closet, all that matters is that someone feels or is perceiving that they are powerless.

When outward expressing people feel powerless, that is against their natural energy. None of us like it, no matter our root expression. Powerlessness is unwanted, and we begin to push against it. We know our natural, healthy, inclination is to feel in charge of our own life, mind, decisions, results. When we are living and experiencing a restriction of those aspects, we need to shift out of that.

An outward expressing person creates the energy of anger. Anger is a good thing, necessary, and beneficial. Anger is rocket fuel to project yourself out of the gravitational pull of powerless. Anger is vital for that huge push away from powerless.

The problem is, none of us are taught what anger means. What causes it. Where it belongs. How it is good, and how to use it for good. By its very nature, anger is not engaging the mind, and not clear thinking. Anger is a pure, raw, emotional state.

Even more important to understand its place and its effects *before* you are in the middle of it. Anger is not the time to open your mouth. Anger is not the time to engage your fists, the knife, the gun, the axe, the car. Anger is not the time to confront anyone. I mean, anyone. Even if you are ten thousand percent justified in holding them responsible for your anger, and even if in some form they deserve your wrath.

Anger is a heads-up that there is something really important to you and that thing made you feel hurt, or powerless, or like you weren't in the decision making position about your life and this circumstance. Anger is the signal that you are ready to move yourself into a place you prefer. So, get good and pissed off. Blame everybody. Blame me (god knows, others have). Blame your great aunt Millie. Blame every person who ever lived.

Just don't take any action toward the object of your blame. Let it flame out, and get your thinking started. Smart thinking. You and your situation clear thinking. You and your situation you are responsible for all of it, thinking. You feeling back in power and capable, thinking. Which releases that need to blame others.

Is it easy? Absolutely not, at first. It's as foreign as if I asked you to knit a winter scarf or sing Christmas carols as soon as you get angry. Is it worth it to learn about your emotions, your feelings, and the way you operate as a healthy person?

Seriously? Of course, it is.

When we showed Jake his strengths, and that his natural, powerful, outward expression is his benefit, he was more able to understand Maggie and her natural inward expression. He was perceiving her quiet, withdrawn, and accepting reaction as some form of validation that he was correct in his insecurities. When he realized that the insecurities were minor, at the start, and from issues he had from his own collected experiences, he was able to sort all of them out and release them.

Most people on the delivery end of the abuse have something - a voice, a feeling, an inkling, that their abusive reactions are wrong. There are exceptions to this rule, when the powerlessness and collected anger cycle is so strong it never rests. However, in most all the cases I've examined and people I've worked with, they have their own cycle of guilt and self admonition. But, because they don't understand why they said that, felt that, did that, behaved that way, it only ads fuel to the powerlessness and guilt. Their own guilt and self blame for their actions actually increases and intensifies instead of soothing and easing.

Jake was able to take care of his reasons for feeling powerless from all of his personal life directions causing the insecure feelings and beliefs. That, alone, reduced his level of anger. He understood what anger was, with him personally, and developed means to use it to his advantage, instead of to harm someone else. He learned to heed the warning signs that he was starting to venture in to insecurity and powerlessness, his triggers, so that he never got to the point of needing the rage type of anger. As he learned about himself, and took control of responsibility for his own mind, feelings, emotions, thoughts and actions, he rarely got to the out of control anger stage, again.

Maggie was able to see how her pulling in and hiding was harming her on more levels. How each of them, simply behaving according to their natural root energy type, but not being aware of and understanding those types, was escalating the problems. Maggie, when in her powerlessness, could not get angry. Anger is not a place we inward moving types go. We get a version of angry, but we can't get to blameful, to really letting our anger for the situation and at another person, or group of people, increase to the point of moving us up and out. Up and out just isn't our thing.

Maggie needed to discover how her own powerlessness and insecurity displayed. How it pulled her deeper within. It took away her strong power - her ability to think, to figure out, to evaluate details.

Once we discovered the healthy balance in their natural original expression, everything changed. Forgiveness wasn't easy, scars do remain. We don't get over what happened, none of us, either deliverer or receiver. But perspective and feeling safe help tremendously.

The Four Origins - SuzyQ and Paul

Let's understand the basic dynamics that are in play in this relationship.

SuzyQ, being a naturally buoyant and upbeat root engagement type, simply doesn't stick with perspectives and feelings opposite or opposed to that energy. She can't. It's almost physically impossible, if not emotionally impossible.

We needed to get Suzy to come to terms with how wrong it was for her family, teachers, and parents to treat her they way they did when she was such a little girl, and through school. That her reasons for leaving high school were to avoid undergoing mandatory drugging to settle her down. We explored how her parents, no matter how misguided they were and how abominable their treatment of her, were doing the best they could with the information they had. Neither parent wanted to drug Suzy, either, and they just didn't know her superpower was her lightning mind, her ability to see ideas, solutions, directions, that none of the other types can.

Her type is best suited at keeping this light, which is not to say lightweight or without value, more the fresh, uplifting energy balance. Each of the four root origin types has a strong suit in a different direction and expression than the others. SuzyQ is meant to lighten up the downward pulling Maggies. To bring sweetness and laughter, joy and pause to the outward force of the Jake's. To draw out the solid still wall within that is Paul.

SuzyQ is designed to see possibility. To see new horizons, ways and ideas and new concepts. To be unrestrained by convention and previous pattern, so we can move forward in new directions, not become stagnant. With her decidedly up, light, fresh full ideas, to ask her to then take one or two singular ideas and bring them down to carry out would be like popping every balloon that is Suzy. She would wither and fall to the ground.

SuzyQ's job is to hand off all of her ideas, all of the new, all of the weird and wonderful and untried, to the Maggies. Maggies are consumers of information and data. Maggies take all those ideas and add detail, give them roots, develop them into plans. Maggie's turn SuzyQ's apparent scatterbrain into coherent, workable, detail laden, projects.

But, then we expect Maggie to take those projects and make them 'go.' Turn them into something tangible, bring them to fruition. Those are outward expressions, the antithesis of Maggies. That isn't Maggie's job. Maggies job is to hand off the detailed plans to Jake.

Jakes don't really feel comfortable with a lot of deep detail and experimentation, research, study, introspection. Jakes are built for taking the ideas that were shaped into good plans and bringing those plans to life. Jake takes the intellectual work from Maggie and makes everything into something we can see, feel, tangible, results, finished.

But, then comes Paul. Paul is the cool cucumber. Paul has the root energy superpower of evaluation. Paul is an inward pulling energy, but his is vertical inward, the opposite of Jakes wall of motion forward. Paul is a solid wall within. Paul doesn't deal with the detail and constant motion of evaluation that Maggie has. Paul has the superpower of evaluation, of critique, of criticism, to see what and where needs improvement and correction. That is why Pauls exceed in mathematical constructs and concepts.

Pauls are usually not comfortable with the inner evaluation of emotion, nor the outer heat of passion. It isn't that Pauls aren't loving, they are. It's just that Pauls love from their heads. Think Spock. Pauls are not burdened by the emotion of needing to take care of anothers feelings, so Paul can just tell it like Paul see is it. Straight, no chaser, no filter. If Paul was a nurturer, like Maggie, Paul would hesitate in sharing his clarity that there was something wrong which needs repair. Now, would be good.

A Paul in balance is awe inspiring. Paul's, however, out of balance, have that challenge of not being able to really understand emotions and emotional reactions. Pauls are often thought of as autistic. They are very comfortable in their head, observing, commenting, sharing whatever it is that they are considering, and quite sure that they are correct. Which, often frustratingly, they are. Their heat is a cold, icy cold, heat. Pauls also, because of their self certainty, have a bit of a control freak issue when they are imbalanced. A balanced Paul is still prone to believing he's the smartest person in the room, and doesn't really care if others agree, nor not - but the balanced Paul can easily work with others at their level. Again, think Spock.

Paul was able to see that the very thing he was criticized about, and bullied horribly for, as a child was actually his strong suit. He was knowingly taking his insecurity and self doubt, from his unbalanced place of navigating life, and unleashing it on SuzyQ. He did feel guilty and self denigration when he hurt her as he did, and that fed his spiral, as well.

When we try to discover the imbalances they have, Pauls are difficult to work with, in the beginning. After all, Spock knows everything. You have to work pretty hard to earn the respect enough of a Paul so that they will hear you out, try on your words and concepts. Paul genuinely did love Suzy, and he was able to grasp, immediately, that his behavior was not okay, so was intense and intent on discovering how to right himself. Pride, self regard, and it flat out made sense to him.

They did not stay together, but ended with both helping each other heal and balance. Last I heard, Paul was working with other Pauls who are out of balance, helping them in ways only another Paul can. Suzy is still getting to know and accept herself, taking longer to work through the negative from her past, because she just doesn't like to revisit it or linger.

Next Steps:

To listen to audio, watch a video, or sit in - as my guest - on my next web masterclass about how to find your own root tendencies as well as how to see the behavior of others you need to be aware of -

- ◆ On the web, go to http://fourrootorigins.com/lisalfour
- ◆ On your smartphone, text LISALFOUR to 12264551275, and an invitation link will be sent back to

you immediately
♦   Or, simply scan the code below from your smartphone:

Shadow and Light Lie #3
"She Has A Restraining Order, It's All Good"
And
"The Courts Are Involved, So I'm Safe, Now"

Elyse had made it out of the house with her bathrobe on, and not much else. She hadn't dried off from her shower, much less grabbed undies and the like. She scooped up her three kids as she ran out of her home, not stopping to look at anything but the front door. She knew if she didn't make it out that door in the next few seconds, she might not make it out, at all, unless to the coroners office on a gurney.

The baby was screaming, pudding from dinner still around her mouth, her diaper dirty. The twins, Diane and Dane, were in cotton PJ's, barefooted. Harry was cleaning up the baby and the other kids from the evening meal when it started. He was being very nice, most of the night. It was his idea that Elyse take a nice, hot, shower to transition out of her stressful day. It was a bitch of a day at work, and she was exhausted, tense, and raw.

She was careful to disguise those feelings, not to do anything which might set Harry into one of his binges. She could smell the vodka on his breath. Harry had this game he played with himself where he believed drinking vodka left no telltale scent. He was wrong. Elyse had worked a double shift at the Post Office in Canada. Tensions were high, there was a heated management/worker situation, escalating by the day. On top of that, it was freezing nasty cold out.

After letting the shower run over the knots in her shoulders, she had that sense. Just the foreboding and intuition which comes from living in the war zone of domestic abuse. Something was coming. She could feel it. Quickly turning off the water, she grabbed a towel and her bathrobe. It was then she heard the sound of chairs smashing in the kitchen, and what sounded like dishes shattering. All she could think of were the kids. The baby was in the kitchen.

Dropping the towel to the floor and hastily throwing her robe around her, she raced out of the bathroom to the highchair. Harry was lifting each dinner plate, one by one, and breaking it forcefully against the sink. She couldn't tell what he was muttering, but she could see shards of glass flying around the kitchen, some very near the baby. Taking a quick glance to make sure where the twins were (trying to hide behind their bedroom door), she made a leap for the baby.

Harry turned just in time to see Elyse lift the baby into her arms. He knew by the look on her face that Elyse was running. She stopped only for a second to realize she was barefooted through some of the ceramic shards on the floor, blood showing on her pale skin. She wasn't sure if it was that sight which put the idea in Harry's mind, or just coincidence, but Harry looked at the huge piece of jagged plate in his hand, and gripped it tighter, like a knife. He set his gaze on Elyse, and lunged for her face.

Elyse, buoyed by adrenaline and sheer terror, started for the front door. Both twins stepped out and reached up for her, with Elyse managing to get them both in one arm, although Dane was hanging by his pajama tops in her hand. He reached up and grabbed on. Harry was close behind, weapon still in hand.

Elyse made it through the door, and down the front porch steps before Harry made contact. The sliver just cut through her robe, grazing the back of her neck. A neighbor was just getting out of his car, witnessing the events, he could only begin screaming.

It was enough to stop Harry for just a moment before he lunged stronger at Elyse. She had tripped over Diane's tricycle in the darkness and slippery cold sidewalk, the blood on her feet acting like slick oil. Had she not fallen, Harry would surely have put the shard directly into her back.

By then the neighbor was close enough to pull Elyse out of the way, and grab Dane. The kids were screaming in terror, along with the neighbor. More lights came on, more neighbors watching. Harry had slipped on Elyse's blood, losing the shard of weapon as he fell. Elyse was almost to the open door of a neighboring house when Harry stood, again. Harry was calling to Elyse, threatening to kill her, and the neighbors for interfering.

Elyse and the kids were taken to the emergency room, and then she decided to go to a shelter, rather than put the neighbor in any danger. Elyse was embarrassed, humiliated, scared and coming down off of a powerful adrenaline rush. She and the kids were freezing, confused and terrified. Harry had been bad, before, but tonight was worse than she ever imaged he could get.

Through the next weeks, Harry turned himself in to authorities, apologetically. He agreed to start counseling for domestic violence issues. He entered alcohol abuse treatment. Elyse found a duplex on the other side of town, a nice quiet street where the kids could play and she didn't have to look the neighbors in the eye. She bought furniture, and began sleeping at night. Almost.

The kids were still a little shellshocked from the trauma, but Elyse and her family - her younger sister, her mom and uncle - were helping out and making this a big, new adventure. At 4, the twins were old enough, yet young enough, so it was helping. Elyse, and the family, sighed a huge breath of relief the day the judge handed down the restraining order on Harry.

He was to stay at least a block away from Elyse and the kids, at all times. He was not to contact Elyse under any circumstances. Harry was to have highly restricted and supervised short visits with the kids, one at a time, in a court designated safe place. Harry agreed, and honestly told the court, as well as his counsel, that he would honor the Courts' demands.

There was much ease and a bit of normal life settling in for Elyse and the kids. They developed a smooth routine. Even started to laugh, again. She loved those kids, and she was feeling hope that life was finally turning out well.

Until the night Harry decided Elyse was his wife, and those kids were his kids, too. What right did any court, or judge, or an outsider have to tell him he couldn't have what was his? Harry told the police he had brought the gun with him only to protect himself in case they wanted to arrest him for seeing his family. He wanted to threaten Elyse, to get her to listen to reason, that was why he brought his loaded gun.

He didn't mean to kill Elyse, the baby, Diane and Dane, Elyse's sister Gail, and uncle Jason.

No, Harry did not mean to kill them, at all. He wasn't sure how it turned out that the gun he was holding had discharged into each of them, several times. Harry was sorry. He loved his wife and kids.

This is one of the most dangerous lies we have when it comes to domestic violence. It's the lie, so widely held in our society, that for some reason when a man who has been abusive is handed a restraining order by a court of law the man will honor and obey that order.

For the life of me, I don't understand how, or why, we believe this.

Fair warning, this one really gets my feisty going.

We put laws in place to stop people from doing something. Laws are written for people who would never break the law in the first place.

That logic. We create a law to stop a person, or people, from doing something. And, then we expect those people to stop doing that something, and say "Okey, dokey, I won't do that any more...since it's a law, now, and everything..."

Why? That makes absolutely no sense.

We cannot legislate common sense. We cannot enact enough laws to give anyone morals. We can't hand down court edicts which give someone compassion, a clue, intelligence, awareness or a sense of the right thing to do. Even our contracts are only as valuable as the intent of the people who sign them.

In the case of domestic violence: we have a person dishing out the abuse.

There is a problem there, with the abuser. A problem the abuser has in thinking that this kind of abuse is, by any means, okay. A problem in self excusing behavior. A problem in justifying behavior.

Abuse is, at its core, entitlement. The abuser believes him (or her) self to be entitled to engage in this activity. Its okay with them. We never, ever, do anything we aren't first okay with, in our own minds and hearts.

Whether it be opening our mouths to hurl insults and angry words; whether it be use our body to inflict harm; whether it be to use a weapon to inflict harm; no matter how it is we are inflicting harm - we have made it okay to do so.

To take a person with an imbalance so much that they find it okay to inflict abuse on an intimate partner and simply, albeit sternly, tell them to knock it off and stay away because it is a law, or a court order....then expect that person to simply do as they are told...that is the height of lunacy, to me.

It doesn't work. I don't know why we expect it to work. I suppose because we use the word 'law' and law enforcement is involved at some point.

But, in the case of domestic violence and that particular dynamic, unless there is an officer accompanying the abuser, and the abused, 24/7, then the restraining order edict is doomed to fail.

Fail, it did, on Elyse and her kids.

Am I suggesting we don't hand down restraining orders and restrictions? Absolutely not. Of course we should. They are necessary parts of the equation. Every now and then they serve as enough impetus to shift a safer outcome.

What I am suggesting...no...begging, pleading, stating, admonishing... is that we all stop regarding the restraining order as something which provides actual safety and resolve. Too often women and their families regard that restraining order as some sort of science fiction shield which will protect them. They believe that their abuser will actually honor it. Or, if the abuser shows up, they can simply call the authorities, and the abuser will be dealt with, swiftly and surely.

Those scenarios are absolutely not true. She is not safe. The abuser will likely not honor the order, but test it, push it, perhaps escalate the violence because of it. Law enforcement can't be instantly present when the (hopefully unarmed) abuser arrives.

Safety in a restraining order is an illusion, and it's a lie we must be rid of.

Shadow and Light Violence Pattern #3:

Elyse thought:

- I moved, Harry will have a hard time finding me;
- Harry won't push the boundaries, not after what happened;
- I have a restraining order against him, he knows that and doesn't want to go to jail, so he'll obey - I know he will;
- Even if Harry slips, law enforcement will be here and arrest him, again…so it's okay. We're okay…safe…

You think:

- She's out, she moved, the crises is averted, all is well;
- Harry's not that bad a guy, of course he will stay away, he doesn't want trouble;
- She has a restraining order, the courts are involved, that's a big deal, it's okay;
- Law enforcement will take care of it, now, because of the order, so she is safe;
- Since a woman I love is going through this, it's good she has the restraining order and protection, now…so she's okay…

Understanding, seeing clearly, why Elyse would have felt she was safe - between moving and the all powerful restraining order - helps all of the Elyse's I've worked with, and those of you women reading this who are recognizing you are Elyse.

It also helps you, those of you who know and love an Elyse, begin the process of unraveling this set of dangerous lies.

The Living in Shadow and Light Truths we need to hold are:

For the Elyse's:

- Harry just might be more angry that you moved, slipped out of his control, trying to assert your own power. Moving is good; believing he will be good with your moving is dangerous;
- You got to this place to begin with because Harry pushed boundaries; Courts hand out restraining orders only with good cause; 'good cause' means Harry doesn't care about boundaries; Harry is lost in whatever he's doing to justify this, and the court can't change that... but until Harry changes Harry - he will continue to push boundaries - your boundaries
- Harry probably knows that domestic violence and abuse on this scale is frowned upon, and he probably knows he's in trouble for what he's already done; Harry, in that frame of mind, is most likely going to ignore a restraining order, or deliberately violate it to assert his authority with his family, again; you are **_not_** safe because of the restraining order
- Law enforcement has much to do, and often is somewhere far from you while engaged in other law enforcement activities; even when law enforcement commits to respond quickly, sometimes that just isn't quick enough; and please, be honest with yourself - it

isn't fair to depend upon law enforcement to be there instantly if Harry shows up. You can, and should, be taking steps to make sure you are responsible for your safety, first - and that is a huge difference from your receiving abuse mind set, but vital...and you can do it...

For those of you with women you care about:

- She might be out, and that crisis averted, but the dynamic hasn't been changed, and their relationship hasn't been dealt with; if anything it's been aggravated and will get worse
- Harry might not be that bad a guy; Harry just might respect the Court and the order; but Harry thought it was okay to do something so dangerous, illegal, immoral, unethical and outrageous that he was slapped with a restraining order in the first place - so how about, for safety sake, we don't depend on Harry to see the error of his ways? How about we be intentionally proactive to protect the ones we love?
- Again, to put all of the responsibility for her safety, her family's safety, on law enforcement isn't practical, and it puts a lot onto them; they do a great job, but cannot teleport instantly or be half a block away at all times; be thankful for law enforcement - yes, absolutely - but do not put all your safety eggs in their basket; take care of it yourself, as well
- This is someone you love, you care about; she's likely experiencing PTSD and the effects of abuse, so don't rely on her to be able to make sure she and her kids are safe. She just might not have what it takes, just now, and will need your wisdom and help. With her, not for her; support, not force. But be proactive in her situation

We can explore how we reached this disastrous point, for both of them, for all of them.

Shadow and Light Better Questions #3

"If the restraining order isn't the beacon of safety and security we want it to be, what in the world do we do?"

"If I can't count on that restraining order, and I'm really not safe, maybe even in more danger than before, what in the world do I do?"

Taking it from the point of my rant, above, and how the people involved were falsely believing in safety, the better, stronger, and more reliable answers would be developed at the time, for individual circumstance.

Ideas and strategies which have been successful include:

◆ Creating your own version of witness protection;
◆ Using a private system based on the old 'underground railroad' so the family is impossible to find
◆ Making sure that patterns are interrupted, so Elyse and the kids aren't easy to find at 11:27 on Wednesday morning - because they are in the same place every Wednesday morning at 11:27 AM

The last is the most difficult, it's hard on 'normalcy' and routine for the kids...but the thing you want most is to make it difficult, if not impossible, for Harry to find you easily.

You cannot rely on Harry, the Court, and law enforcement, that order written on a piece of paper. Don't violate the rights of Harry and his kids - don't break the law yourself and make it worse on everyone. But do find ways of preventing Harry from easily finding the family.

Enlist the ear of womens shelters, their advice and networks. Of retired law enforcement, their advice and suggestions. Of others who survived domestic violence, their advice and suggestions. Take action to keep yourself, your family, your loved ones, safe and away from Harry's reach, at all costs. Start conversations in neighborhoods, at workplaces, at schools and at shopping centers.

Talk about it, ask questions, get ideas, come up with plans which work for everyone. Pro-active, making yourself and your kids important, safe, is the most vital focus.

This takes a village, and it takes everyone being smart, ethical, within the law and creative to make sure Elyse's, Diane's, Dane's, sisters, babies, aunts, uncles, moms and dads are safe, healthy and alive. Pull together. Don't push at Harry, focus on all of you, safe.

Next Steps:

To listen to audio, watch a video, or sit in - as my guest - on my next web masterclass about how to find strategies to be safe and protect yourself and your family-

◆ On the web, go to http://domesticviolencesolutionsalliance.org/protect
◆ On your smartphone, text PROTECT to 12264551275, and an invitation link will be sent back to you immediately
◆ Or, simply scan the code below from your smartphone:

Shadow and Light Lie #4
"He's In Jail, So She's Okay"
And
"Well That's Over, I'm Okay"

Mark was sentenced to 15 years in prison for what he did to Jennifer.

To look at Jen, you can't see any evidence of Mark, the abuse, or the years of torture he inflicted. There are no scars, no visible remnants.

Jen was great, all through the trial, the appeals, and the sentencing. It was difficult for her, constantly reliving the horrific events, but she held up like a trouper. Every now and then she would sort of shut down, check out, and hole up in her house. But, then, she would be back to 'our Jen' in no time.

Everyone admired her for that, would tell her how proud they were.

There was much self congratulation amongst Jen's supporters when Mark was, at last, sentenced and shipped off to prison. Release, and relief, with the agreement about how everyone can get on with life and put this nasty, painful, time behind them.

What they missed were the signs that Jen was anything but okay.

Jen's scars were on the inside. The damage was in her mind, in her heart, and in her spirit. Jen was able to put on a good face, after all, she practiced that through her darkest times with Mark. Never to let anyone on the outside see what was really going on… her "game face," she used to call it.

Now, her game face was part of her every day face.

Sure, life was calmer. More peaceful. She wasn't wondering if she would be murdered in her sleep, or maimed, tortured, or tied up, raped and sodomized repeatedly by Mark.

But, that sleep, it still wasn't showing up. There was no sleep to be had, really. She would break out in sheer panic and sweat, for seemingly no reason, at all. It was difficult to keep food down, and sometimes it would be a few days she had to go without nourishment, the vomiting was so severe.

Was she talking to herself? Sometimes there seemed to be a screeching sound in her head. Not in her ears, in her very brain. Jen told me it reminded her of an old western movie, when the train is squealing on the tracks, metal against metal, as it grinds to a stop.

She even found herself snapping at little, odd, things. The peas in the wrong slot in the grocery store. Why should she suddenly have great irritable passion about a can of peas slipping over to hang with the chili beans?

What most people believe is that, after the hubbub and rigamarole, sentencing, and calm after the storm, she's okay.

All done.

Because what most people don't understand is partner violence, that abuse in a relationship with someone you love, someone who tells you they love you, someone close to you…that kind of abuse effects and damages a woman on deep and lasting internal levels.

She ends up with the most potent displays of PTSD (post-traumatic stress syndrome). She doesn't know that is the problem, and she likely isn't aware of the depth of her problems, all around. To Jen, these new life displays seemed random. Weird. More anomaly than pattern. Life after abuse is so very different, in all ways, in all moments, every night and every day, that what should give us pause or cause alarm can simply seem like a natural part of this very different day to day existence.

When we got together that afternoon, she was gracious. Gracious in a kind of clunky, funky, quirky, way. It was genuine. Jen was lanky, pale skinned, brown eyed, with just a hint of copper in her brown hair. A couple of freckles on her nose, even. She smiled quickly, and naturally. But, you could sense, and see, the slight mantle of tension lifting her shoulders. It was evident in subtle ways, if you were looking - like how she was perfectly relaxed, laughing, joking - suddenly turning serious and very concerned that a throw pillow on the loveseat was upside down. No. No, that wasn't right. It had to be 'just, so' before Jen settled back into being Jen.

The prevailing belief that she is out of harms way, time to put all that nasty abuse behind and move on, is highly faulty.

There were hiccups in Jen's life navigation skills which got her into an abusive relationship, in the first place. Those navigation skills were further damaged, tweaked, destroyed and obliterated as the abuse continued.

Now that it's over, there is no Genie in the Bottle showing up to correct, right, fix and repair those skills. She likely doesn't realize that her initial navigation skills were faulty to begin with, much less way out of whack, today.

Then, the actual abuse and its after effects, on top of her

navigational imbalance. Between the two, she is not near whole. Jen is far from healthy, self reliant, and able to care for herself.

And she has no clue this is happening.

When we are - all of us - you, me, every man and woman alive - are in an intimate relationship, a form of coupling relationship, our emotions are involved. The love/in love/lust feelings, thoughts and emotions are prevalent. When we are at work, these three are usually not at play with an argument, even bullying. The added psychological, physical, emotional and mental components of a romantic relationship, or 'family,' are complicated.

Even what we call a 'normal' run of the mill relationship has difficulties. Coupling gets us at our most vulnerable levels - no matter what your root engagement type.

The violence and abuse in an intimate relationship muddles our ability to define the abuse. The common view from the outside, that what goes on in a relationship is none of your business, or that couples yell and fight and say horrible things to one another as normal, add to the blurring of the line where domestic violence begins, how we define it.

The lines of acceptable are pushed. Often, non-existent. The relationship turns into a war zone, but this war is within your own home, in your bed, in your bathroom and kitchen. It surrounds you at all times. You never know when the attack will begin, nor its severity. There is no intel or observation to see likely movement and firepower from the other side. There is no way to defend, nor to hide. The war of domestic violence is in the foxhole with you.

There become areas of predictability, such as there are limits of what the abuser will do in public. There are some predictors, such as whether or not alcohol, drugs or other external factors are added. As a victim of domestic violence, you do begin to get a sense of when the attack might be set off, or detect signs of the beginning. Still, this largely just alerts you to the situation sooner, and does nothing to avert or deter, stop, interrupt the violence. If anything, it adds to the anxiety of the victim because they know it's coming. Anticipation of the violence, bracing yourself for it, as well as the futility of our mind scrambling to avoid it but realizing we cannot, only serve to make it worse.

I'm often asked to compare the trauma of domestic violence to the more traditionally accepted models of PTSD and Stockholm Syndrome, and Jen is a good example to illustrate this difference.

Trauma, when used in relation to PTSD, is accepted as a type of anxiety disorder. It can occur after you have gone through an extreme emotional trauma that involved the threat of injury or death.

It's most widely used in terms of war, veterans who have served in active duty. It also is widely applied to any event where victims have been subject to an unexpected violent attack. What comes to mind are school shootings such as Columbine and the more recent Sandy Hook. When violence, death or the threat of death, are thrust upon you, usually by a stranger.

The very description of PTSD can't equally be applied to domestic violence, though the media and some professionals in the field of psychology attempt often try.

The stress involved with the continual, constant, and unrelenting threat of injury or violence in a domestic abuse situation is compounded by the fact it is someone you know, someone you likely care about, and someone within your home. Even in date or more separate personal relationships - the 'personal' is a huge factor.

This violence and threat is coming from any direction, at any time, but by someone you know and care about. Someone who might care about you. The anxiety factor is multiplied in ways we still cannot clearly define. There isn't a lot of research into the effects of trauma within a domestic violence relationship, but from my experience, it is just as deadly.

With PTSD there is clearly a 'post.' The soldier returns home. The shooting at the mall or school is over. There is an 'end point' which we can clearly see and agree upon. The threat, itself, is removed either by removing the person from the threat or the threat itself ending. Then we can clearly deal with the after effects, the trauma caused and the injury to mind, spirit, emotion.

In the case of domestic violence there is not a clear end point. He might be in jail, or incarcerated. That is a clear removal of the threat. However, since the threat is personal, as long as he (or she) is alive with the remote possibility of being able to reach the victim, it is not over. Not even remotely over.

The abuser is still a very viable threat, unless the abuser is dead.

The stress and trauma from the day to day violence has shifted, but if there is any way for the abuser to be in contact with the abused, the threat has escalated as it shifted. Now our semblance of safety in predictability, and our experience of going through the violence, has been removed. If he (or she) has simply been separated from us, we don't know when, where, or what will show up into our lives as the violence. We are on high alert at all times.

We are dealing with the 'post' from what happened in the relationship; we are dealing with the 'present' in that simply because he was told not to or incarcerated doesn't mean he will not pick up where he left off; we are dealing with 'future' because we have no idea when he will show up, be released, decide it's again time - or not.

We are in immersion stress, and the anxiety wreaks havoc on our lives, our ability to make sane and good choices for ourselves.

Domestic violence isn't something that happens 'to us' - as if it is asserted upon us or takes us out of our day to day lives. Domestic violence comes as a part of the relationship we have, from the relationship, itself. Domestic violence becomes part of the fabric of that relationship, and a normal part of our day to day lives.

We, as victims, and those of you who love us, need to address:

- The realization of the depth and impact of the trauma which was the violent relationship;
- Discover the underlying reasons and factors which are a part of us which got us into that relationship in the first place, and repair them
- Deal with the after effects, the clear 'post' trauma from the relationship;
- Learn, discover, be aware of the current, different trauma, threat and anxiety - how it shows up, how we experience it, and get a good system for offsetting it, managing it, healing it
- Learn, discover, be aware of the practicalities of the future, honestly and on the side of caution, for the trauma to continue - and how we can prevent or minimize it, so we can feel safer, more secure and more

in charge of our own life

- Overall, learn, understand and be aware of how we move through the trauma, our anxiety, its appearances on that highly individualized level in each life

The Stockholm Syndrome is often mistakenly used in relation to domestic violence, because on the surface there are similarities. The basic characteristics of Stockholm are related to hostage situations, and where domestic violence seems close to a hostage situation, it is not.

Stockholm Syndrome displays:

o   The hostage has negative feelings and beliefs about the police or other authorities
o   The hostage has positive beliefs and feelings about their captors
o   The captor develops positive feelings about the hostage

Usually this is resulting from an intense situation lasting longer than a week; the captor shows some kindness to the hostage; and there is continuing contact between captor and hostage.

The similarity, and I believe the base cause of mistakenly contributing Stockholm Syndrome to domestic violence cases:

- Both hostage and victim of abuse have negative feelings or beliefs about police or other authorities
- Both hostage and victim of abuse have positive beliefs about the captor or abuser
- Both the abuser or captor has positive feelings about hostage or abused

Where the Stockholm model is drastically different, and so ineffective as a model for healing domestic abuse trauma is in the basis of origin.

Hostages are 'taken' by strangers. It is a surprise, the event asserts itself in to the life of a person taken against their will by someone they don't know. There might be the slightest awareness between captor and hostage prior to the act of containment, but there is no relationship between captor and hostage at the outset. The relationship does not shift from friendly and acknowledged into one of captor/captive.

The aspects specific to Stockholm Syndrome result out of that basis: people, or a person, unknown to the hostage begin the interaction with the hostage in a traumatic and anxiety inducing way by the very nature of the 'taking' of the hostage.

In domestic violence, it begins as a relationship. Two people know one another, and voluntarily begin interacting with one another. The positive feelings precede the violence.

The other vital difference is captivity. The hostage is forced, forefront, and aware - at least initially - of the unwanted and unwelcome captivity. Through conditioning in the hostage situation, or in kidnap, the captor asserts more control over the actions of the hostage and the hostage is not continually physically confined.

In domestic violence, the conditioning is forefront. There is no realization or awareness of captivity in either abuser or abused. They have a relationship, and that relationship has parameters which include silence, rules of when and how the abuser and abuse live physically, but it is not based out of force initially.

The other factors, such as kindness, affection, and negative feelings of authority are products of the captor/hostage situation. Kindness, affection and contact are where the abusive relationship begins. If anything the abusive relationship moves the other direction from Stockholm

Syndrome.

The basis for avoiding police and authority in protecting the abuser - your spouse, your mate, your lover, on some level your intimate partner - are complex and arise out of not only your loving/kind/emotionally romantically attached relationship, but also the natural factors of protecting a loved one. These reasons are more than skewed, and exceptionally unhealthy, but it doesn't seem like it from the inside.

The trauma of domestic violence cannot be adequately explained using models from these two prevalent systems. The domestic violence victim has many layers of trauma, mental, emotional, physical (directly from the abuse, or as a result of the stress and anxiety of living through the abuse, most likely a combination of them both).

Shadow and Light Violence Pattern #4:

Jen thought:

♦ What a mess, I'm so glad that's over and I don't ever have to think about it, again;
♦ Life is 'normal' now, he can't hurt me, so I can move on;
♦ I'm probably just tired, I get exhausted so easily;
♦ If I can get some sleeping pills, get some good nights sleep, I won't be so jumpy and I'll be back to normal;
♦ I'll just wait this out, it will take care of itself after awhile;
♦ I'm completely free of Mark, and everything that happened

You think:

♦ I am so proud of Jen, she was made it through to the

other side of this;

- It's good to see her getting back to normal;
- She seems tired, a lot, but that's probably to be expected;
- Perhaps a good prescription for sleep will take care of it;
- The guy is out of sight, far away, and gone - so she is okay;
- Her nervousness is to be expected, after what she went through, it will take care of itself

Understanding, seeing clearly, why Jen would be experiencing these seemingly random displays of distress shows similarity to all the Jen's I've worked with, and those of you women reading this who are recognizing you are Jen.

It also helps you, those of you who know and love a Jen, begin the process of unraveling this set of dangerous lies. These are the kind that lie in wait, traps set to keep Jen in turmoil and anguish.

The Living in Shadow and Light Truths we need to hold are:

For the Jen's:

- It's great to celebrate 'making it through' and finding that place where you are safe from abuse; but it's not time to go blithely into 'normal' until you have discovered what a healthy, whole 'normal' would be for you, given what you've experienced;
- No organization or system has really achieved any significant research on the after effects of domestic violence and its associated trauma, so we aren't talking about how you are very likely experiencing mild to severe symptoms of PTSD - and that, in itself, is 'normal'
- Everything you went through, all those days and nights,

took its toll on you. Your emotions, your thoughts, your feelings, your body, all have been through indescribably difficult stress and injury - even if you can't see it. Take the time, the focus, to discover what your mind, heart, body, spirit is trying to tell you - how you are out of balance, and take the steps to let yourself heal on all levels. It, whatever is going on, won't go away by itself, in fact it might get worse and show up in a way you want even less. Learn to take care of yourself, and this is a great place to start.

- Give yourself the gift of discovering your own 'why' that put you on this path; what beliefs did you hold that started you, and held you, in a relationship that was so intensely damaging and dangerous?
- He might be physically absent, but he is almost part of your cellular and emotional makeup, due to that intensity; simply because you remove yourself from the front lines of the war doesn't mean you are home free - it means you take the front lines with you wherever you go, inside;

For those of you with women you care about:

- There is a woman you know, care for, and love, going through this - so you can learn how to be someone she can confide in
- There is a woman you know, care for, and love, going through this - and you can help her discover what she needs to feel safe, to be aware and alert for the signals where she is experiencing her PTSD, her imbalance and the trauma signals - so she can discover and create a new, healthy 'normal' based on moving forward in awareness
- This is not about 'it will all go away in time' - it's about being aware of what is shifting, what is growing and

what she has come to accept as part of normal life that might not be a healthy part of normal life; no relationship or emotional state 'goes away on its own' - and this is no exception

◆ Be gentle with her, and don't push her to let it go, or to get on with things. Don't encourage that because you might be helping her stuff her emotions ad thoughts down, to run from her own symptoms rather than be able to heal them and deal with them.

We can explore how we reached this healthier point for Jen.

Shadow and Light Better Questions #4

"If it the woman I care about is out of what I think is the danger, and she's probably dealing with trauma caused by this relationship, how can I help her?"

"If I'm facing the after effects of trauma and damage from my relationship, and it isn't okay simply because he's in jail and I think I'm safe, what do I do to start to take care of myself?"

Next Steps:

To listen to audio, watch a video, or sit in - as my guest - on my next web masterclass about how to deal with the after effects of trauma and domestic violence, for you or a woman you love visit

- On the web, go to http://domesticviolencesurivors.org/ptsd
- On your smartphone, text PTSD to 12264551275, and an invitation link will be sent back to you immediately
- Or, simply scan the code below from your smartphone:

Shadow and Light Lie #5
"He'll Never Change"

Through the hundreds of women I've worked with in the last 20 years, I find that they make up about 95% of the participants in the domestic violence relationship who reach out for help.

But, now and then, that other 5% is the man.

The man delivering the violence. Or the man on the receiving end. Here, though, we'll talk about the abuser.

It's exceptionally difficult for men who are abusive and violent to shift out of that. Particularly to speak to a woman about it. There is that primal, man-woman thing (and in this instance I am restricting this discussion to the traditional male/female violence loop).

That basal mating instinct - hormonal, conditional, societal. It involves our animal, deep brain, and chemical reactions within us, so this isn't intellectual, thought, practical, reasonable.

We have that cave-man and his cave-woman sexual interaction at play.

This contributes to one of the other Big Lies - which in this book didn't rate it's own page though still vital for discussion- "It's personal between a man and a woman - what happens in a marriage or relationship behind closed doors is really none of my business."

That's a convenient lie, from your outside point of view. Because in your relationship, marriage and behind closed doors you aren't threatening, being threatened or the rest of the gamut that is domestic violence and abuse.

Behind our closed doors, however, that same lie kicks in, only used differently to reinforce and justify the abuse.

That sense of entitlement. Of property. Of our myriad definitions of relationship and marriage.

Often we even give a bit too much slack for, say, an argument between two people that gets heated, a bit out of hand… that isn't too far fetched. Even in your own relationships, words are thrown, tempers flare, perhaps a glass or two is hurled against the wall. A slap across the face of partner or mate, delivered in the heat of anger and frustration, well deserved by the receiver, that's not a big deal. Or, so we justify. It's passionate. And, there was an apology.

Look at the film "Mr. & Mrs. Smith" with Angelina Jolie and Brad Pitt. Their now infamous 'lovers spat' where they literally destroy their home. It's sexy, it's hot. No one denies that. The passion is palpable, exciting. Assassins trying to kill each other, but mates playing the mating game, interwoven in all those intimate partner relationship shades and textures.

Not that we are taking submachine guns and machete's into our domestic violence disputes (although, some are). Their interaction hot and sexy and passionate and tension breaking.

Real world domestic violence is not a meeting of two equals playing with one another in their expertise of choice.

Real world is one asserting dominance, and the other acquiescing, relinquishing self to the dominance and aggressor. Let's not go anywhere near "50 Shades," either. Not even close.

Real world, the man is entitled to yell, use force, hit, berate, humiliate, torture, threaten, whatever he pleases, because this is his.

This, at the point we've arrived, is not a love, not her, not a she, not a name... it is his... The it happens to be a living being, a woman, or a child... but it is not human, it is a possession, property.

He is entitled to do as he pleases, and no one outside that relationship has any right, authority, input or jurisdiction...

That might be uncomfortable for you, but it is the way of life, in here...

So when a man wants to interrupt his own pattern of violence as abuser, that is a big, huge, step.

Bruce and I got together to discover if I might be able to help him. He was my first male. Not because I shunned working with men - I actually love men - but because no man had sought my help.

And, honestly, I wasn't sure I could be of actual benefit. I understand the abusive patterns, see clearly the underlying reasons and causes, I get the dynamic and I tend to stay pretty firm in those as focus.

These help me to stay detached from what happened, and mostly non-judgmental. Mostly. I still react as a woman, and have a momma bear side when I know that someone is abusing a woman, child, animal, where I want to jump in and give back to the abuser in the way he abused. I know it's because this is important to me, and what all of those passionate thoughts, feelings and emotions mean in the grand scheme of things - so I would never take action on those feelings, thoughts or emotions.

But it is why I didn't go through to get my degree in veterinary medicine, because if I knew someone was deliberately hurting an animal I'd most likely come across the counter and go postal on that person.

Today, with someone engaging in delivery of abuse I have intellectual knowledge. I do not know what it feels like, on an experience level, to hurt or harm someone. I, as a person, cannot do it. I know what it feels like to want to, but not what a person must go through to make that in any form of acceptable, much less to actually take action and hurt someone.

I told Bruce, up front, I might not be able to help, and I explained to him what I just shared with you. We agreed to simply walk away - no harm, no foul - if either of us felt uncomfortable, or that we weren't being of benefit.

Bruce was shorter than I, but muscley. We used to call his body type stocky. I looked at those muscles and strength, and admit, my mind ventured into anger that he would use that strength against a woman or child. Even if she were a body builder, not a fair match. I caught myself, after all, Bruce was reaching out for help. It wasn't court mandated (which is rarely effective, and usually backfires abominably), Bruce volunteered.

I gave him big points for that.

Bruce was raised by calm people in a Norman Rockwell kind of family. We were really challenged to see how Bruce went so askew of his base root, which was actually the male version of a Maggie. Bruce was introspective, he loved complexity, detail.

Bruce was also deeply emotional.

There was the key.

Most of us are not taught the difference between an emotion, a thought and a feeling.

It's a tough one, because even most psychologists and psychiatric practitioners can go awry on this one.

We have those three, very different, life states:

1) Thought;
2) Emotion;
3) Feeling;

But then we have to factor in your root origin tendency style:

A. Upward, light, fresh, young, free
B. Inward, rolling, detailed, nurturing, 'classic feminine' attributes
C. Outward pushing, heated, action, activity, tangibles, 'classic male' attributes
D. Inward vertically, still, cool, intellectual, analytical

And, add the final leg of your personal life engagement triad:

- Auditory: leading with hearing, sound, music, words
- Kinesthetic: leading with touch, interaction, full spectrum involvement, sensing
- Visual: leading with seeing, watching, observing

This model differs from the 'four types of engagement' commonly used. The fourth type is often described as separated reading and writing as a learning or engagement style.

I disagree. Reading is visually taking in words, but it is largely auditory. We see the words, but hear them in our own voice, within our own minds. Writing is using words, but it is kinesthetic, where you actually touch the page, keyboard or writing tool, and you are using movement to create your thoughts and ideas into words. I believe that the read/write belong separated into each root - hearing and touching.

We can't begin to explain how you think, how you feel, how you take in, integrate and express life until we have a clear indication on each of these meters.

Your root tendency needs to come first, because, of course it is your root. You may have learned and adapted skills you tried to place on top of your root, to alter or hide, disguise it…so we need to uncover and discover that, first. Then fit your life engagement style with your root.

After we determine your base comfort zone, your root strengths, then we decipher how you process a feeling; a thought; an emotion. There is not a set structure - these are individual matches on the buffet, and highly individualized to you and your life.

I'd love to give you the quick and easy, down and dirty, way to figure this out in 22 seconds, here - but it can't be done.

You can discover it for yourself, it's fascinating and simple when we do it, and I have a program and tools to help you. Yes, this is a shameless plug for my Four Origins System.

It takes a hair longer than 22 seconds, more like a few days, but as hype-y as this sounds, your whole life literally does change. It becomes, for the first time, wholly, fully and completely your life - your home in your own world.

I'm veering from my format for this book, here, by not detailing Bruce, simply because I don't want you trying to fit yourself, or someone you love, into a 'Bruce' from your now perspective. I'd be irresponsible if I allowed or encouraged that.

I will say that Bruce was able to put his own pieces together, discover where he had some pretty damaging misconceptions about who he really was. Together we took each aspect, each concept, Bruce's perspectives, decisions and experiences and put them into the Strategy. He found the areas where he was personally heading in directions he was unaware of, but becoming aware, he could alter and correct.

He worked at finding his own balance, and he was able to heal his own life as well as his marriage. They worked hard.

Men do change.

The ultra important factor here is: it has to come from within them, be their idea; they need to be 'all in' for themselves.

Men, women, anyone, all need to initiate the change from within. On their own volition, in their own way and in their own time. That is why court ordered counseling so usually resoundingly fails. It isn't his idea, it's part of the humiliation and punishment. No one can force another to wonder what is wrong with them, and to be in a place strong enough within themselves to want to find out, much less fix it.

When it is his idea, though - not manipulated or coerced - it's powerful and restores your faith.

Another vitally important factor: when you have gone through the concepts and tools in the forthcoming chapter "We All Have A PoP," you'll discover that the mindset, the emotional place, the thought and feelings needed to take self responsibility for your life and actions can only come about in a person who is not in the middle of self torture.

Recall in the first chapter when we discussed the difference in perspective between you who would not abuse or be violent, and those of us who are in the thick of the abuse and violence? That our experience and ideas and perspective and decisions are so very different from yours because we are in two very different places with life?

With the PoP, and other concepts you are discovering through this book, you'll see the contributing lie with regard to abusers, the lie which is making domestic violence worse.

- He should know better, stop, walk away;
- He should get help if it's that bad;
- He should 'man up' and get some self respect, knock it off

And the like

When, in order to realize, in your own mind, for yourself, that you have a problem - and it's your problem, the problem you are taking responsibility for - you have to be pretty healthy and stable, internally. It takes an exceptionally balanced and mentally/emotionally healthy - not stable, but healthy - person to be able to want to undergo self examination.

Self examination opens you up to seeing your own warts, your own mistakes, your own big screw ups. You have to be in a place where you can deal with that, work through it, not self implode or explode. So a man, or anyone, who is in the middle of unhealthy and imbalanced thoughts, feelings, behavior - as in the throes of domestic violence action - is nowhere near able to take responsibility, see their actions as dangerous, or be involved in their own salvation & healing.   Two entirely different mindsets, places of viewing life.

Anyone can get from disconnect, unhealthy, imbalanced and self defeating to connected, aware, healthy, balanced and stronger. They first have to want to; second have to realize where they are; third have to get a good idea of where they would rather be (since likely they have never been in health, balance and strength before); and get a good plan to move from where they are to where they need to, and would rather, be.

Yes, he can change. He has changed. If he genuinely wants to.

Same can be said for any of us.

Shadow and Light Violence Pattern #5:

Bruce thought:

+ I don't know if I can stop this reaction;
+ I hate myself for what I do and I seem powerless to stop it;
+ I don't know of, or hear of, any other man changing away from violence;
+ I can't tell anyone about this, I'm ashamed;
+ Will it last, can I make it permanent, if I do change?

You think:

+ Men don't stop being violent and angry, they can't change that once they've done it;
+ He should hate himself, it's vile and unforgivable, what he has done;
+ I don't know of any man who has ever 'fessed up to being violent, and changing that behavior, I don't think he can;

- It probably won't last, the guy is violent - it would be stupid to think he will never do it again. Once a jerk, always a jerk;
- Since a woman I love and care about has a man being violent but saying he'll 'change', and she loves and cares about that man, I need her to see he won't/can't change - not really

Understanding, seeing clearly, why Bruce would have felt he couldn't change helps all of the Bruce's I've worked with, those of you reading this who might be a Bruce; and those of you women reading this who are recognizing you are living with a Bruce.

It also helps you, those of you who know and love a woman who has a Bruce, or you know and love a Bruce as brother, son, friend... begin the process of unraveling this set of dangerous lies.

The Living in Shadow and Light Truths we need to hold are:

For the Bruces's:

- You can change anything you want to; you just need the right tools, the best strategy, some proven steps - and some worthwhile experienced advice as you take the steps; you have to own your own transformation - no one can take that from you;
- It's natural for you to berate yourself for your actions, that's actually good. Most men justify their actions, so you specifically holding yourself in error is a good first step. The powerlessness issue is at play in other ways in your head and heart making this thing big and nasty and awful. Discovering your genuine power within it, by its very nature, dissolves your 'powerless'

- Men, by your nature, don't trumpet that they used to be a perpetrator of domestic violence. There isn't a lot of public support for changing that behavior, more public belief it can't be changed. The men who have changed are out there, and it is part of the cone of silence in the whole domestic violence dynamic. Besides, it doesn't matter if you are the only one - as long as you honor yourself and be that one;

- Any behavior, negative or positive, is transient. We constantly either reinforce or discard our choices, our reasons for our behavior. If you choose to make this change permanent, it will be up to you to maintain and sustain it. It, you, your actions, are not outside of your control, even if it seems like it, right now. It's a dangerous illusion. Own your change, your behavior, your deeper understanding and your actions will follow naturally

We can explore how we reached this healthier point, for Bruces'.

Shadow and Light Better Questions #5

"If there is a way I can stop doing this, to change my behavior, to interrupt my actions, what would that be, how do I start?"

"If I know a Bruce, and I am pretty sure he is Bruce in a domestic violence situation, how can I even bring that up, and be a genuine part of help and healing?"

Next Steps:

To listen to audio, watch a video, or sit in - as my guest - on my next web masterclass about how to find how this effects the man and woman you life in their domestic violence struggle, or your own mix in the context of feeling, thinking, emotion; your root tendency; and your style of processing information, visit

- On the web, go to http://fourrootorigins.com/bruce
- On your smartphone, text BRUCE to 12264551275, and an invitation link will be sent back to you immediately
- Or, simply scan the code below from your smartphone:

Shadow and Light Lie #6
"You Are So Strong and Capable!"
And
"I Can Handle This, I'm Strong and Capable"

I was sitting at a table in a little rural coffee shop. It seems I do some of my best work in little coffee shops. I was, for the incredibly uncomfortable first time in my life, firing a client. It was quite the scene. I was apologizing for firing him. I was being a good girl, letting him know why - how disappointed I was that he didn't show up, because he was letting down an entire group of at risk people which really, desperately need his services. But I was doing it in my full blown "please don't hit me" fall back/old mode.

I'm so used to being verbally or physically attacked that I anticipate it at every turn. I'm internally accustomed to being literally or figuratively slapped the very instant I make the slightest attempt at standing up for myself. It isn't a conscious thing.

More like walking, talking and eating, it becomes the fabric of your makeup. Just - normal - because I learned these things at the formative stage as a child, and reinforced them through most relationships into adulthood. Of course, all along the way through life I didn't realize this was happening - we don't, do we? We just live our lives and react to them. But, it was okay. I was strong. I was smart. I was capable, so I could handle it. Even as a child.

Here, in the coffee shop, I was watching myself get small, get apologetic, get very nice and sweet and gentle and I was almost rolling on the table - not even sitting up straight! ... aaaarrrgggghhh! But, I fired him. I bungled the firing so badly that by the time it was done he felt sorry for me. Not what I intended. Yet, I hope not to get good at firing clients. I hope to choose better, going in.

The man sitting across from me was struggling to operate his organization. He was a 'rescuer,' and I am determined to help any rescue, shelter, team, group or organization whose mandate is to move women, children, animals, men, away from their disconnect and into safe, healthy, lives.

Today, this man was moving from a current client to a used-to-be-client. He, for his own reasons, could not show up and be present in his own endeavor. I've had a couple of clients like that. Good, passionate, experienced people who - for whatever internal reason of their own - can't really step up to the plate and be fully there to make a good 'go' of their dream, their passion, their business.

One previous to him was a dear and wonderful friend of mine, a woman I hold a deep fondness for, even today. She's good - really good - in an area the world sorely needs. It combines her life, her heart, her passion and her wisdom. Both of us were depending on her - I could do everything but <u>be</u> her - we built the business around her to support her to be her. She ultimately failed herself by not being able to actually conduct business. I held on, held on, held on...until it took the last of what energy, money, and strength I had left. She was pushing hard against her own internal demons, exhausting herself in the process. Both of us, she and I, needed her to step up and rock her expertise. Ultimately, she just...couldn't.

I understand. I understood at the time. Her own imbalances from her childhood and personal history were at play. In a way, I'm grateful to her, because she was part of a powerful triad of business people/friends I was working with at the same time. My part was behind the scenes, infrastructure, strategy, with each. All they had to do is be themselves, do their thing.

Each could not, when it came right down to the wire.

The invaluable lessons these three beautifully flawed people showed me are an integral piece in being able to be so effective in helping others to help themselves, to understand themselves.

This friend had told me, almost from the first moment we met, the way she believed life to be. In her view, every single person she had previously done business with was a sociopath - a sociopath who ripped her blind, hurt her, harmed her. The stories were heart rending. Often, in her mind, our job was to stop the sociopaths of the world! We would let everyone know how sociopath these sociopaths actually were! It was some work to bring her focus back to the business at hand, which was in many ways preventing new sociopaths before they began.

The second client/friend I was working with used to be an accomplished psychologist. He had isolated himself down, down, down, as well, through the years. Though he still handled a client, or two, it was from his home office via Skype, rather than an active, in person practice. When we first met he told me how he viewed life, the way he believed it to be. His stories, too, were heart rending. Every woman he has ever known has lied to him, cheated him, hurt him deeply, from his mother on to present day. His lovely daughters were the sole exception and he was a bit blinded by the exception he held for them. It blocked his ability to realize they were wonderful women, with challenges, issues and hiccups - and that they needed their dad to see that, to be there for them. He had these two extreme dichotomies. His daughters were perfect. Women, however, the rest of us, are evil, bad, and hopeless, will always lie and will never change.

The third client/friend I was working with was an accomplished businessman at one time. Smart, savvy - the

Paul type of brilliance (from the 'Four Root Origins' chapter and 'He's Not That Bad' chapter). This man was determined to rebuild his life. When we met, he told me the way he viewed life, how he felt, what his beliefs are. His stories were heart rending. Women don't know anything about business, and they should not have anything to do with business. Women in business, and women in general, hurt him, deeply. Women never listen to him, his wisdom, his decisions - and women never do what they are told. That's the way women are. As Paul's, when this root origin type is imbalanced, they can be on the manipulative side. My friend was quite good at manipulation, justifying it in his mind as the ends justifying the means, because to him he was right, he was always right about everything- so a little (or a lot of) manipulation to get others to do what he wants them to was - acceptable. Necessary, even.

My part, in the mix, was that I see the good inside people. I know it's in there. It's often buried under lots of junk and garbage that person has collected over the years. Junk and garbage handed to them along their life path by others. Often the behavior on top of that really great person shows signs of being not-so-great all the way to really-horribly-awful. But, because of my work, I also know that it's simply behavior, and it's simply because they have skewed, unhealthy, ideas and ideals they carry about themselves and other people. Usually, those skewed ideas and ideals about themselves they've comfortably blamed on other people. But the really unique and beautiful person is in there. The true root beauty will come out to play, peek into life, around me. I interact with the beautiful person. It's really fabulous.

The benefit in these relationships, to me, was that I knew I wasn't a sociopath; I wasn't a woman set out to break anyone's heart/lie to them/cheat them; and I was proof in the pudding experience excellence in the business world but in a business sense not easy to manipulate, at all. Personally - easy as pie. In business - not going to happen.

We actually did have some form of that discussion, individually. I commented that they obviously shifted their energy, because they had attracted me, a person who was 180 degrees different from those other negative experiences they had before. How cool was that?

So, it's all good, with each of these people! I clearly was not going to be the type of relationship they had previously experienced.

Yay!

Now, of course, it wasn't as if we all sat down and discussed our "Rules of Viewing Life Beliefs" - that would have been so much easier. We were almost completely unaware we had any "Rules of Viewing Life Beliefs" in the first place.

Instead, as would inevitably happen:

- ✓ She, after moving away from her business, decided that I was just like everyone else - a sociopath; and as a special bonus, I had left some of my personal items at her home while I left the country to take care of other urgent business - and she thought it was a nifty idea to call my other friends and clients - total strangers to her - and repeat her 'sociopath' tale - now including me in her list of sociopaths, all the while choosing to keep my exceptionally personal and valuable things without returning them to me. True to her nature, she chose to share her beliefs behind my back, and now a few years later to the date of publication of this book has not told me to my face. I only discovered her views from my friends & associates after she had spoken with them.
- ✓ My second client decided that I was just like every other

woman - a manipulative liar, and thus refused to pay me for any work I had performed for him. He delighted in delivering his views of my evil worthlessness often, directly at me, in my presence. It was interesting to observe how much he enjoyed that unique kind of cruelty, and how he had chosen to justify his actions and words. He held his PhD in psychology up as evidence and absolution in his need to obliterate any sense of self worth I might have had. It was for my own good that he destroyed me, he was a professional who knew these things, after all.

✓ My third client decided that I was like every other woman - incapable of conducting business, and incapable of doing what I was told. He, true to his root nature, told me, directly, but also chose to share that with a few others. A blend, if you will, of the other two clients. A bit behind the back, and a bit as direct affront. All bases covered.

With my dear, close, friend - her ultimate abandonment of her business sent me into one of the most frightening places I've been. My financial flow was so tied to her success, her following through, when she went on her way my tenuous shoestring existence evaporated. None of those clients paid me for my work, nor did they fulfill their end of the business arrangement. I was left on the hook for ongoing expenses and investments.

As I describe it, I found myself "between homes." I severely downsized my living arrangements, having no other choice. Others admonish me that, technically, I was homeless - because living in the back of my 4Runner cannot be stretched to be called a 'home.' Hey, there was an air mattress in there… isn't that home-y? Home-like? Home-ish?

Okay, perhaps not.

I arrived between homes in fits and starts. It didn't happen overnight. Because, no matter what happens, I'm strong. I'm capable. I'll figure it out. I'll take care of it.

Where, a few years earlier, before the sudden death of my 'what dreams are made of' marriage - the night my husband, playmate, life mate's heart stopped beating - I was pretty comfortable, financially. I had invested well over the years - I'm good at it. We had a nice portfolio and lifestyle. The moment he died, I was plunged into scrambling to rebuild.

But, that was okay. I can handle it. I'm strong. I'm capable.

I, though, was devastated after his death. Only half jokingly I used to tell others that I was afraid I actually died that night, too, only no one was brave enough to tell me that. I felt like a walking ghost of the woman I had become in our marriage.

I was defeated. I was empty and lost and shaken to my core. His death was so shocking and whiplash and unexpected and unwanted and... my 'happy' was zipped into the body bag with him that foggy night, removed from me...for what I thought was forever.

I also quite unpleasantly and equally unexpectedly discovered I wasn't quite broke, but close to it. My financial flow evaporated before the ambulance even got his body to the coroners office.

I could not begin actively teaching, counseling, sharing, again. I could not be there to help others with emotional, psychological and mind troubles. I just didn't have it in me. But I could be 'behind the scenes' and help others do their thing. Do it better, more profitably, more savvy, more sustainably.

But I still had a couple of persnickety little wrinkles, and I was amazingly unaware that they were messing with my life. I was unaware of their very existence, these little wrinkle rascals.

Those wrinkles were forefront in the interaction with these three clients, but I had no idea until much later. This awareness was sparked by a now dear friend, the woman I met in the darkness the night my husband was pronounced dead. She is a wise and intuitive professor of psychology, as well as a giving practitioner in the mind healing psychology arts.

During the aftermath of these three business/friend disintegrations, I was trying to make sense of it, them. I still don't understand what process another human being must go through in order to actually choose to take action to deliberately hurt another human. I just couldn't do it. It's my 'outside looking in.' I would hurt myself, deliberately, long before I would consider harming someone or something else.

Why? Why deliberately act on a choice to hurt another? Particularly another person who trusts you not to. It's one of the most basic aspects of domestic violence relationships, this choosing to and taking action on, deliberate harm. It's a common thread in many relationships throughout my life. I needed to discover the clues, the answers to this riddle.

And then, I did. As most discoveries, once you become aware of them, you can find it so clearly all around you. You get it, and it sounds so right. It all clicks into place.

In all my years of counseling, of teaching, of uplifting and rescuing, I didn't realize that we tell one another the way we think about what life is. As with these friend/clients, I didn't realize, at the time, that each was telling me the way they need to view the world. The decisions they had made about others, and life, and relationships, and money, and business.

I don't mean the normal way we share our feelings and beliefs about life, what we think. Those delicious philosophical and practical conversations we have about 'life.'

No, I am referring to the deeper, undercurrent, layer beneath in our stories of what happens in our lives. Not the story, or event, itself - but the way we frame the event, in our mind. The conclusions we decide about other people, and how they are cast, their character, in the stories of our lives.

In the case of my three, with their stories of what happened previously, each was telling me distinctly the structure they built in which they feel comfortable. How they shaped their past into a pattern which would keep repeating.

One - everyone in business is a lying cheating low life sociopath out to hurt her; one - women are lying, cheating, manipulative vile little creatures who are out to hurt him; one - women are flighty, unreliable, undependable, necessary evils who don't belong anywhere around business or relationships, and never do as they are told - and every business relationship is manipulative - just the nature of 'business.'

This was the way each formed decisions about what had happened to them previously. Each lived in those decisions as a way to understand & accept their life experiences, everything that had happened to them. So, moving forward, each would have to find a way to have every new relationship fit into those belief systems.

That was their gift to me, and to this work. It has been a invaluable piece of the puzzle of 'us', you, me, communication, life, healthy and healing.

After I made this powerful discovery, I revisited my research and work, as well as previous relationships of mine, I was able to clearly see, easily detect, how every person would tell their views of life, and 'other,' in their stories of what happened to them previously - but the real meat and substance could be found in the decision they hold about those 'others.' We only had to learn to hear, to feel, to listen - and there it would be.

It's shifting from hearing "this is what happened and what this person did to me" into "this is what I believe people do in these circumstances." Huge differences in the value of what is shared, particularly if there is a pattern and the "what these people did to me" is repetitive.

It helped me, going forward, avoid such bitter entanglements as these three turned out to be. I learned to discover my own view of life, of people, the structure I've chosen in which I need to have everyone fit: that everyone belongs here; everyone has a root which can be found, nourished, healed, restored; the person might believe they are junk, but I don't believe life makes junk; everyone has value - even if they don't know that, or behave like their true value, just now...

I can hold these views and decisions because they are meaningful and important to me, but I must then blend my decision with listening to their overriding and most prevalent idea of Who They Are: someone who needs everyone to be a conniving sociopath; someone who needs every woman except his daughters to lie, cheat and manipulate; someone who needs every woman to be a waste of time and trust all the while he is perfectly justified in being manipulative; and such.

This was huge. Yes, the person I see, I feel, I know to be good and valuable is still under there - but I could now temper interaction with them by understanding that they just might not see what I see in them. They might have a stronger and more practiced view of life that is harmful, dangerous, painful, and that needs to be respected in any interaction. It's their filter, their lens, and their structure...everything, including me, must fit their structure. Just as I was fitting each of them into my "you are good, wonderful, valuable and awesome" belief system and structure.

Though I was in my super micro-mini-home, I knew I had some major issues within myself I needed to address, finally. My dear friend/client who needed me to be a sociopath, she was a surprise, I admit, when she decided I was just like everyone else. I hadn't seen that one coming, not at all. It stung, deeply. And it was she I referenced in the preface, my stinging wounds, just wanting to retrieve my vulnerability and fade into my shadows, invisible, to heal.

During this technically homeless time I was still counseling those coming out of domestic violence relationships, as I could. I was so empty, so alone. So self doubtful, so unsure of my ability to judge others on a personal level with any kind of accuracy. There were days I didn't eat, because I needed to make my $20 last for a week, or more. A burrito every other day was sometimes 'it,' nourishment-wise. The 3 for $1 kind in the frozen section of the grocers. Did you know, if you buy frozen burritos and put them on your dark gray dashboard in the sun for a few hours they get nice and warm enough to eat? I didn't. But, I did discover that. Now, you know, too.

My mother and my sister, the only family I had left, had died in quick succession on the heels of my husbands death. I have a wonderful nephew - my sisters son, brilliant, unique and I adore him - but we hadn't really spoken in awhile. Because I'm close to a Maggie-type, I pull in. I don't share. I don't talk about my problems, or what goes on. I just...don't. I'm also a slight blend of 'go get things taken care of' type. Ponder, detail, formulate, decide - then take action to make things work. But that 'make it work' on a personal level had long ago been so damaged and beaten as to be left on the wayside in disrepair and disregard.

By all means, under no circumstances, ever, would I ask for anything. Not ask for help. Not ask for one solitary thing. I learned in early childhood that to ask for food, clothes, help to clean my banged up knee, help with homework or...help... under any circumstance...meant a nasty retribution price to pay in return. Asking for help - you might, maybe, slightly maybe, get the help - but there would be more than a pound of flesh to pay for that help. It was also just as likely that any requests for help, no matter how important or vital, would be ignored - and you'd have to pay the piper the pound of flesh or more simply because you asked. If you'll excuse the mixed metaphor, there.

The don't ask combined with the don't stand up for yourself is how I formed the basis of my unbalance: I'll figure this out for myself; I'm smart, I'm capable, I'll be okay - no matter what, I can figure this out. Do not, Self, under any circumstances, seek help. Never. Never. Do not stand up for yourself and expect to be respected by someone else - not going to happen. The other person will attack you, and it will get worse. So, shut up, go within, and figure it out for yourself. You're smart. You are strong. You are capable. You can figure it out, Self.

Those childhood years taught me I was worthless. I was worse than worthless - I was a burden and a nuisance on deep levels. My mother had gotten pregnant with me so she could trap my dad - a man almost half her age - into marrying her. When the romance was not what she hoped she openly regretted not aborting me. I was a reminder of her broken dreams, a competitor for my dad's affection.

My half sister, from my mothers previous marriage, was 10

years older than I. Innocent, funny, gangly, sweet. Tall, beautiful, painfully shy. And every night for eight years, until she left the house at 18, my father would come into our room after arriving home from the bar at 2 AM in his drunken stupor to sexually molest this sweet girl. We had twin beds. I processed it all into monsters chasing us at night, some very nasty nightmares. My sweet sister wouldn't even cry, because she didn't want me to wake up. She just took it, in silence, every night.

My sister never got over it. She did tell our mother, though. Begged her to intercede, step in. Begged our mother to allow her to go live in the country where she was raised, she could stay with our grandmother, mothers mom.

Our mother turned a deaf ear to my sisters pleas. My sweet, beautiful, sister turned inward on herself and started on her own journey of being abused by men in intimate relationships. She shut down, deep within. She could never pull out of the damage. She, too, had learned that no one would care how deeply she hurt, or that she needed help. She, too, had learned that those who tell you they love you will harm you, denigrate you, or ignore you completely. She, too, learned that if you stand up for yourself there is a potent price to pay, in return, so best not to. After never having experienced any kind of happiness with a mate she finally succumbed to uterine cancer in 2010, on Thanksgiving, her favorite holiday.

I took all of this, for most of my life, as my fault. Had I not been born, my dad would not be delivered to the gates of hell to rot in eternity as his highly judgmental religion demanded. I was conceived during an illicit affair between he and my mother while she was married to my sisters dad. It was quite possible her divorce from my sisters dad might not have been exactly legal. Which meant it was also quite possible that his marriage to my mother might not have been exactly legal.

Which meant it was also quite possible that, despite their last minute scramble, I was born illegitimate. He lied to his own parents about the whole thing, until standing with a newborn daughter in his arms was too difficult to explain away. In his world, he broke about 7 of the Big Ten, commandment wise. Not good. Quite sordid and biblically epic, you know. Had I not been born, or had I been successfully aborted, my sister would probably have had a pretty good life; my dad would not face gods wrath by the hand of the devil himself; and for many other reasons the world would have been better off without me.

Childhood taught me to isolate. To be quiet. To begin the skills of invisibility in order to simply survive. Not to let anyone see 'in here,' nor ask for anything, from any one, at any time. To keep my mouth shut so I didn't get punished, slapped or publicly humiliated for speaking my mind. To be self reliant, even if I had no clue how to proceed. But, I'm smart, I'm capable, and I would figure it out. More often than not, that motto served me well.

In teen years my parents returned to the rural community where they were raised, away from my comfort in the big city where I was born and raised. High school brought overt and outright bullying, not only from students but from faculty, It was hell. Ever increasing powerlessness. Just keep my head down, mouth shut, and make it through.

Relationships, as an adult, were mildly unhealthy increasing in intensity to dangerously so. When I was thirty I found myself alone. Lonely. I had been working in an intense job as a high ranking bank officer, interfacing with the federal government at top levels unraveling complex real estate portfolio issues. I loved it, but it consumed my days and nights. Literally, three years went by and I hadn't even been asked out on a date much less had one.

There he was. Now, I'm 5 foot 12, stocking feet. In heels, 6'3" ish, and I love my heels. Tall, you might say. I turned around, at the car wash no less, and looked up into the most beautiful blue eyes I had ever seen. The face was gorgeous, crowned with Elvis black hair. He was 6'4" of delicious yum, and I was a goner.

His life had been difficult. He was much younger than I. He had suffered his own abuse from parent, grandparent. He had gotten into trouble, minor scuffles, with some angry outbursts. I saw the kind, warm, tender, wounded man/boy inside. Inside this incredibly breathtaking package, mind you. I had not learned the lesson of 20 years later, to hear how a person views life because they will need to fit you into that view. Oh, how I could have used that knowledge with this gorgeous man/boy.

Over the almost immediate next months I became pregnant. I was on the pill, and it was more than a surprise.

He had been slowly and systematically cutting me off from my friends, which, with me, wasn't difficult - I had a handful at most, and his comfort was my first concern. His jealousy and insecurity began to rage.

I was sicker than a dog with morning sickness and still taking the pill. I wasn't sure why they call it 'morning' when for me it was 24 hour a day sickness. I knew I was pregnant, and for 5 months each test came back negative, so had medical personnel telling me I was imagining the pregnancy and it was likely a side effect of the birth control pills combined with stress. They would adjust the type of pill, yet the symptoms continued. I wasn't getting bigger, I was almost skeletal. I was losing weight with not being able to keep anything down and his violence. I felt trapped. But it was okay. I was strong. I was capable. I could figure it out.

When, after all the months of false negatives, we finally received the positive test he changed. There was the man I saw inside…the violence ended, and all was wonderful. We 'did the right thing' and married. Less than a month later I was in the emergency room, not directly due to his violence, but my body was shutting down. Malnutrition, stress, high fevers, my kidneys were failing. I needed to make the impossibly difficult choice to end my pregnancy, because my baby, my fetus, was damaged beyond repair and would not develop. I was dying, and they were doubtful of my recovery with anything less than dialysis and kidney transplant.

Those days were sheer hell. His violence was back with a vengeance. I had my surgery in the Bay Area. I, the only one in the facility, 12 hours after the Loma Prieta earthquake all but destroyed portions of San Francisco. The aftershocks were powerfully destructive, yet we could not postpone the procedure. Part of me wished that one of those aftershocks would just kill me, too. I believed this was a good time to die.

My husband had fallen into the habit of punching holes in walls, denting cars with his fists. For years, at least once and often several times a day, he would pick me up by my throat like I was a little rag doll, slam my head against the wall, his face inches from mine as he told me the creative and torturous ways he intended to kill me. No warning, he would go from nice and gentle to slamming me against the wall in under three seconds, flat.

He would shake me until I collapsed, telling me I was worthless and a piece of garbage.

No one knew. No one outside the relationship had a clue. I'm smart. I'm capable, I'm strong, I can figure it out. Don't ask for help. Don't stand up for yourself. My motto, words to live by.

I couldn't call the authorities, he begged me not to. He had been in juvenile detention several times. He couldn't go back to jail as an adult. On that, I agreed. Those stints did nothing but make the problem worse. He learned to be tougher, not smarter. He learned to be meaner, not gentler. He learned to be angrier, not wiser. They didn't teach him to understand and get a handle on his anger and outbursts, they taught him how not to get caught. They taught him how to feel worse about himself as a human being.

He also began reinforcing 'don't tell' with the "if you do, I'll kill you..."

One of the big lies about domestic violence: for you on the outside it's a no brainer that the man, the perpetrator, be punished. He knows right from wrong. They are his actions, he is responsible for his actions, he must pay the price for his actions. Done, fini, end of story.

However, to him, living in his twisted self justified version of 'it's okay I treat you this way' - there is no price, retribution or responsibility.

If he gets caught - elevator video surveillance aside - the only way he would get caught is if the woman, in this case me, tells someone. He certainly isn't going to tell anyone. Therefore, if someone in authority discovers this, I did it, and in his mind everything which is going to happen to him by the law and authorities is my fault.

It's our fault. The receiver, the victim, the abused. It's our fault he got caught. It's our fault he is humiliated, embarrassed and treated badly. And we will pay for our mistake, dearly.

A few years into this relationship it was my mothers birthday and I had thrown her a big party. Downtown, her favorite place. It was uncomfortable, her ever present digs at me through that false smile of hers. Seeing my sister growing increasingly more timid and withdrawn by the day, wanting so badly to be loved and give love, but so unable to realize either one. My husband becoming ever more jealous at imagined flirtation directed my way from some hapless, oblivious, cowboy. It was torture, tedious, and when it was over I had decided it was time to find a way out. Away from both my husband and mother.

In the car, about 10 pm, he and I were heading home. Busy traffic, this was a thoroughfare, 3 lanes in our direction alone. The speed limit was close to 50 miles per hour. And he started. Accusations, vile sexual slurs and scenes of me and whomever that cowboy was. He was slamming his fist into the car, the roof, closer and closer to my head. I couldn't do it, not for another moment. I was done.

I didn't look at him, I just quietly said "I want to get out of the car, please pull over." He asked me to repeat it. I did, calm, soft, quiet, sane. His intensity increased, fist faster, harder, closer, I could feel the rush of air as he pushed it up nearer my face. He grabbed my hair, forcing my face toward his, screaming "You want out of the car....????"

"Yes, please, let me out of the car..." I whispered.

Before I knew it, his hand was off my head and on the door handle. In one swift move he opened the car door and shoved me out, still traveling 50 miles per hour.

My base operating system kicked in. I remember looking at all the headlights of oncoming traffic, as I was now facing directly in the path of all the traffic which, moments before, was following behind our car. I thought: "I can handle this, I'm capable, I'll figure this out" - before my feet crumpled under me on the road and my head smashed against the asphalt, knocking me unconscious.

When I aroused consciousness I opened my eyes. It was dark, night, but I couldn't see. I blinked, hard, several times, thinking that would fix the problem. I panicked, but I remember in the oddity of the moment it seemed like in the 70's when you would slap the side of your television to get the picture tube to 'wake up' and come into focus. Funny, the way the mind works in times of trauma.

Slowly images returned. I was mortified to see a large streetlamp on the sidewalk - how did I get to the curb on the other side of those three lanes? ...and faces. Strangers, faces, looking down at me with concern. I wanted to vanish, to blink my eyes again, twiddle my nose, and disappear. Oh my god, there were people hovering over me as I lay crumpled in the road, up against the curb.

For some ungodly reason I started screaming for my husband. I needed out of there, away from their gaze, shielded from their eyes. A voice said that they had called an ambulance, I should stay.

Stay? Ambulance? Are you out of your mind? First, I needed to hide. Second, westernized medicine is not something I find works for me. Third, I needed to hide. Ambulance? No way. All of these words screaming in my head as I stood in outward silence.

I stood up, somehow, and started walking to the car about half a block up. I saw behind me that there were about a dozen other vehicles parked in the road, with a lineup of other cars, still running, headlights on us, backed up behind them. Holy shit, I had stopped traffic, blocked the road. No, I needed to disappear, and nowwouldbegood.

It was difficult to walk. Looking down I saw my sandals were in tatters, dangling from my ankles and dragging the ground behind me, and my feet looked like Shrek. Odd, I thought.

At home, I walked up stairs and looked in the mirror. Oh, no - I had dirt all over my face, my arm, my shoulder. I got in the shower and scrubbed, scrubbed, until I started vomiting. I crawled into bed, and noticed the dirt hadn't come off. My head felt as if it weighed about 75 pounds. I needed sleep.

I woke up the next morning and was fine. At least, I thought I was. In the light of day, I could see that I had bones sticking out of the top of my feet, both of them, even through the swelling. The green Shrek color was nasty bruising beginning to show through the skin. I was dizzy, like the time I had mixed rum and champagne (don't ask...), having to sleep holding on to the floor because the earth was topsy turvy. This time wasn't alcohol as I hadn't had even a beer in months.

But, it's okay. I'm capable. I'm smart. I'll figure this out.

My 'figure out' wasn't working. I couldn't remember my mothers birthdate, though it was the day before. I couldn't remember my last name. Weird. My sister came in, and I could tell by the look on her face that I was in bad shape. Interesting that I needed to pick that up from my sister, isn't it? She insisted I go to emergency, "get my feet fixed, and..." her eyes were brimming with tears...

"And, what...?" I asked. "Just, please, come with me..." was her trembling reply.

In the emergency room I began to shake. I was freezing, as if from the inside out. My skin felt as if it were being shrink-wrapped, tight, painful. I was taken into a private waiting room, laying on my gurney. What was my last name? My sister had just told them. Why couldn't I recall? I closed my eyes to concentrate.

I heard scuffling, heavy footsteps, and a touch on my arm. I opened my eyes to see the kind, very gentle, very concerned faces of two CHP officers looking down at me. One had tears in his eyes. This was not good, I had law enforcement feeling sorry for me. Not good! For those of you non-Californians, CHP is California Highway Patrol. They have jurisdiction over roads and traffic when on a highway or outside an incorporated area. The incident was just outside of town so technically under their bailiwick.

These kind officers quietly, tenderly, asked me what happened. I couldn't say a word. Not because my mind was faulty, I simply would not/could not speak. I couldn't say it, not to anyone, not out loud and certainly not to them.

They knew. There had been several reports of a woman being shoved out of a moving vehicle the previous night. She skidded face first, unconscious, across three lanes of traffic until she came to rest in the gutter next to the curb, her face and shoulder bearing the friction. She was almost run over by several vehicles. She matched my description, my injuries. Wasn't there anything I wanted to say?

I started to cry, and just shook my head 'no.' Little did I know until that moment, that for all these years neighbors had been calling in reports about a man screaming and threatening to dismember his wife, at my address. The descriptions of the wife seemed a lot like me.

They knew. People knew. Strangers, knew. After several minutes of their attempts to get me to confirm this man was my husband and I was the woman he was seen shoving out of the car, followed only by my tears and silence, they left. They could do nothing, take no action against him, without my admission of everything which had transpired, witnesses or not.

I was then examined by other emergency surgical teams which had told me that the 'dirt' covering my face, shoulder and arm was actually imbedded tar where my skin had eroded away. The tar would be there and I would be scarred for life. "Road rash" they called it. Usually motorcycle accident related. They couldn't set the bones in my feet - too much swelling - and the bones would need to heal on their own. I'd likely never walk properly, again.

After my CAT scan the neurosurgeon wheeled me in to show me the results. My skull, my head, was cracked, deeply, in two places. He explained that in the area of the fractures my skull, the bone itself, is actually twice as thick and dense as a 'normal' skull. I knew that, in a way, as it was from the time during pregnancy my mother was trying to spontaneously abort me by surrounding herself with cigarette smoke and cats - two environs where she was drastically allergic - but I stayed put in the womb, only bouncing my skull against her ribs and pelvis, thickening it up a bit.

At that moment I was grateful for the twisted events with my birth, and my mothers unique brand of insanity, which actually saved my life.

They sent me home with instructions on what to do if my concussion worsened, which would signify my brain would be bleeding and swelling was increasing. I'm not sure I understood, what with the concussion, but I agreed to be aware of warning signs. I did understand that my head injury was severe, and that there was the very real possibility I could die as a result. That's okay: I was strong, I was smart, I could figure this out.

It would be another week before my brain function kicked in enough to remember the word 'dermatologist' - I knew I needed to see a skin specialist, but could not, for the life of me, remember his name or line of specialty. He worked wonders, helping me save my face. We made it up as we went along, I was human guinea pig on Hail Mary tries...but it worked.

Today there is virtually no evidence of the severe carnage of that night. The last remnant is from a surgical procedure I needed to repair some of the damage around my eye. I look in the mirror, every morning, and see the scars, the reminders. They eyes looking back at me are different, the eyes of a woman who was almost killed by her husband. Not my eyes.

During the aftermath post emergency room, I couldn't care for myself or walk. It was agony to crawl to the bathroom when I needed to. My whole body was in severe pain. My head was so heavy and so painful I cannot describe the constant misery.

A couple of days later my husband came in and thanked me for not reporting him.

He reached over to touch my hand. I pulled away. I was broken. Broken in soul, broken in spirit, broken in will, broken in body. When he crawled on top of me I began to cry. How could he be sexually aroused at this, me, like this? I tried to fight him off, but - with what - how... All I could do is sob in pain with each thrust.

At that moment I felt more like used garbage than ever before. As he finished, zipped, and left the room, I knew I needed a better plan to get out.

There were many reasons I did not turn him in, some of which I detailed previously, throughout this book. Mostly I knew that he would be bailed out in about thirty minutes if he was arrested. His family had wealth and prominence in LA. I knew he would make a bee-line directly back to me and that the ensuing torture would likely and probably result in my death. I was not figuratively helpless, I was quite absolutely literally helpless.

As soon as it was possible, I made it down the stairs without crumbling in pain. That was the time. I grabbed my two cats, my grandmothers crystal (brain injury: that seemed like the best idea at the time, honestly. Cats: yes; crystal: huh?) I ran. I made some of those colossal mistakes in trusting others, resulting in the one man I did trust twisting my desperation into an elaborate insurance fraud scheme, where he attempted to frame me as a drug dealer (I'm not for a moment kidding... the girl who won't even touch an aspirin, much less drugs...I refused pain killers at the hospital - pharmaceuticals and drugs, poisoning my body - altering my mind and perception - no no no no no! Not my root engagement and life habit...I need to be strong, to figure things out, in control of my faculties at all times).

I was arrested, based on his lying to police and capitalizing on inside-law-enforcement friendships as well as his celebrity (the man committing the fraud was a drummer from one of the most famous bands in the world - prized gold records hanging on his office wall - it's actually one of the reasons, in my half operational concussion addled brain, I trusted him).

It was all quite sordid, fantastical, weird and terrifying.....including SWAT teams showing up outside the house where I was trying to hide and heal from my husband and my trip out of the car. I learned much from this interaction and terror. Not the least of which: don't give yourself a home perm the night before the SWAT team arrives and you get your mug shot taken.

The Steven King meets Dickens? You have no idea. I'm not going to delve further into that nightmare, here, but there is more about it at the link below. Not to hide it, I promised to stay open and authentic, the details of this aspect of my story are just too long and off point to be included, here.

Fortunately the investigators at the DA's office realized I was a tad addled, had found out what happened to me mere weeks previously, and decided to take a little deeper peek into what was really going on. The drummer-turned-accuser was discovered, his pretty elaborate insurance fraud scheme uncovered, and the DA himself apologized to me. I had spent Christmas alone and isolated in jail, terrified and not understanding what was happening, or why. I was just glad it was over, and wanted, as I do, to just put it behind me as quickly as possible.

I took my cats, a small suitcase, and drove away. I had lost my grandmothers crystal after confiscation in the hubbub of arrest. I guess that's where they thought I was hiding the drugs. Doesn't everyone hide a meth lab in a picnic basket? After it was over, I thought I would have loved to have been in the room when they opened their prized 'evidence' and found only a 50 year old picnic basket with a few precious-memory champagne glasses.

The moment the charges were dropped, apology delivered and accepted, I was running, again, and still. There were those surrounding me with encouragement to sue, to demand reparation from the hell the police and courts put me through due to the false accusations and their failure to investigate. But, no - my learned and tightly held motto: Don't stand up for yourself; Don't fight back; Don't demand to be respected and acknowledged.

Just put your head back down and pull your invisibility around you once again.

No, I ran. I ran far and fast. However, we can run, but we can't run from ourselves… I just wanted to die.

After floundering for another year, or so, I landed at the coast, in California. I wanted my childhood, my past, all of the torture and pain and agony and damage to just go away. I wanted me to go away. Since I couldn't kill myself, I did my darndest to obliterate all I could of my life. I wanted to erase my childhood, my relationships, my pain and my worthlessness. I wanted to erase the victim-ness, because even though I didn't feel like a 'victim' - I believed I was garbage and this sort of thing happens to garbage.

I legally changed my name, started over, and tried my best to be someone different. Someone who wasn't worthless, damaged, garbage. At least the intense law enforcement focus bearing down on me for those months had served to get my violent husband to choose to stay away from me. I could go outside, go shopping, buy groceries, be alone, without being on the alert that he would be behind me, across the street or around the next aisle. And I could begin divorce proceedings without fear of being murdered for the choice.

It didn't last, of course, as he grew brazen, again. But, for a time I could breathe.

At the coast, rebuilding…that's when I met the love of my life and we began our magical fairy tale 'happy ever after' for almost ten years until his heart stopped that night. When we fell in love, I told him of the whole rigamarole, sordid and weird, wild and humiliating, series of events that were my past, my life so far. I wanted him to know. All of it. He needed to hear it up front so when he discovered how messed up I was he could decide to bail then and there. I didn't want us to be even deeper in love and out at a restaurant or movie in fifteen years and hear any of this stuff from someone else. He needed to know, and he needed to hear it from me.

He was amazing with it. With me. He was an indescribable part of my being able to heal so much, on so many levels. He was the first person who ever made me feel as if I might just not be a total waste of oxygen and space. He showed me genuine, whole, and complete love in all the senses of the word.

Come now full circle in this chapter back to just a couple of years ago, living in my mini-home, semi-starving, and unable to take care of myself in the most practical sense.

There was, in my daytime safety, a charming man. He was a former military genius spy turned Monk. Honesttogod. I've had the most fascinating experiences.

He finally coaxed out of me the answer to his 'why are you sitting here in the same clothes every day looking pale and scared?' At the time, I was fresh on the receiving end of the 'sociopath' rage my friend had delivered behind my back. I had gotten in trouble with the law for sleeping in my car. The few people only days prior I had counted on as friends had shown me that they were not. I was trying to make it through today. Just, today, that's it. So I could figure things out.

He was also quite brilliant in human interaction, needed for his spy craft days. Accurate applicable psychology was invaluable to him, necessary. He calls his philosophy "DisEndarkenment" and I cannot wait until he publishes his works to share with the rest of the world.

He provided the final key to the whole puzzle. After hearing about some of the 'high points' I've shared with you here (okay, perhaps 'low points' is more accurate - I just prefer 'high points' and 'mini-home' to 'low points' and 'homeless'...), he slapped his knee with his hand. An obvious 'eureka!' moment.

"You have no trust/threat system!" he exclaimed.

I replied with something scathingly intelligent, like "huh?"

He explained to me that I had an inability to register if a person was a threat, or safe. He made sense, it was logical, and obviously proven in his life and teaching.

I balked. Argued. Fought. My mind, my makeup, the decisions I have made about people and life: people are good, valuable, worthy, necessary and beautiful - I could not conceive of 'threat'.

Who goes through life looking at someone else as a threat, nor not? That's not who I am, it's not comfortable, nor even something I could see myself doing. It did not fit with my view of life: people are good, valuable, worthy, necessary, beautiful beings - who just might be a threat? Doesn't fit.

But the seeds were planted. It became the illumination for realizing I like what I've decided about my life, and people, but I did need to factor in the information from the person when they told me the way they needed to view their own life and other people. Respect that.

Had I this information earlier I would not have gone into business with any of those people. I would have seen their true perfection, root tendencies...but realized that those root tendencies were buried and obscured by their need to see others as some form of negative evil. Seeing both, my clear knowing how amazing the person really was, inside - mixed with their clear belief that others are lying cheating sociopaths out to get them - I would have been able to protect myself and respect that they would place their views, first, foremost, and strongest.

I began the process of healing my own inner imbalances, and take back my life - or take it and own it fully as mine - for the first time. Iron out these newly discovered wrinkles which had been delivering such a whollop of an impact throughout my life.

I stopped running. I faced each event from my past to get a better understanding of it and discover its lessons. I made what peace I could with my parents, and others along the path.

I stopped running from myself. I decided to use my own system and tools to heal myself, restore and nourish my own roots, and balance my strengths. Accept that I have non-strengths, and that's okay. I just need to be aware of them. And the non-strengths in other, beautiful, wonderful, people.

I changed my name back to the name my father gave me at my birth. Roxanne.

Though it took almost three years, I made it. During the worst of my mini-home, semi-starving, time I also met several people who were kind, loving, and generous to provide a hand up for me. These people were total strangers to me, introduced by a man I held as a trusted friend. They helped me to get back on my feet, find safe and warm places to sleep, and to put food in my mouth. I am indescribably grateful to these people, and will forever be indebted to them for their generosity. They went a long way to restoring my faith in others, in life, and in myself.

And now, we come back to where we began in the preface.

I don't want you to read my words, to soak in my story, because I want you to focus on me. In fact, in case you haven't picked up on it...I'd just as soon no one focused on me. My shadows, thank you, fit me well.

My preference is you read my story, and I included it last for a reason, with your newfound ability to being understanding the underlying contributing factors of domestic violence, and the women we love, from the inside.

That is my 'inside.' A good look into it. So, I'm trusting (there's that concept, again!) that you - this person I don't know, and can't see - are able to start stepping away from your 'outside looking in' judgement and decisions about domestic violence. I'm trusting that you can now understand it better by coming inside, with me, with the others whose stories I've shared with you.

Tip of the iceberg? Yes.

More to do? Absolutely.

But, together, we've make a giant leap, and a great start toward having those better questions, with deeper answers, to form more powerful, effective solutions.

The woman you care about, the one you have had that gut feeling, that sense - the one you can see is hiding it - you just know that she is in a dangerous relationship.... you might not know how violent, how demeaning, how dangerous - but you <u>know</u>...

She has a story, too. She might not know all of the touch points along the way from her life experience, she might not be able to recognize them and put them together in her tapestry of events leading to where she is, today. But, the story is there. The client I spoke of in the beginning of this chapter, the one I fired? I related a bit of my struggle to him, in explaining how it was important he be present for his business - if he could not, I needed to move on because I was rebuilding my own life.

He sat looking at me, incredulous. His words: "I can't believe that these things happened to you. You seem so strong, so capable, like you would never be in such a bad place in your life."

So, the women around you, like me, might not look as if they are in such a bad place in their lives. We are so very good at hiding, masking, putting on the brave face. Please, don't dismiss the woman who needs you simply because you, from the outside, think she is fine, capable, strong and has the world on as string sitting on a rainbow.

She does not. She has her story.

It's the discovery of the story, looking back, with wiser eyes, with a more seasoned voice, getting the clues from a different perspective - that is what will allow her to see her own story. Discover her own imbalances, and where the seeds of that imbalance were planted. How she can go about healing not only the imbalances, scars and pain - but nourish her natural tendencies and strengths.

Domestic violence, the participants, don't suddenly arrive at a point of full blown violence. Domestic violence and abuse grows from many little seeds nourished. The momentum builds, dig after dig, ding after ding, hurt after hurt, reaction after reaction.

We need, she needs, to be able to get to a place where she can see, feel, hear and know her own story. Only then can she own it, and not feel ashamed. I admit, I do still feel shame, embarrassment, humiliation, in my story. Not as much as last year. As long as I'm gentle with myself, be less hurt when someone chooses to beat me up about my past, I'll feel less shame, embarrassment and humiliation next year. My history and path are mine mine, I own them, and until I accepted them I could not heal them.

The woman you love needs to take similar steps. She can be whole, even if, right now, she hasn't any clue what that means or might look like, feel like, or sound like.

Shadow and Light Violence Pattern #6:

I thought:

- People are really inherently good, honest, and beautiful;
- Why on earth would anyone want to hurt me?;
- I do not, at any time want to cause harm to someone else, even if you - outside the situation, believe they deserve it;
- I'm capable, I'm smart, I'll figure it out
- Never, under even the most dire circumstances, as for help in any way shape or form

You think:

- People hurt other people all the time - they aren't good, honorable and beautiful;
- People hurt one another every day, all the time, its what we do;
- You would tell me to stand up, fight back, don't take it - that the other person deserves retribution;
- That I do, actually, seem smart, capable - so how in the

world did I make these odd conclusions and self destructive decisions?;

It also helps you who find yourself like me, and those of you who know and love a woman like me, begin the process of unraveling this set of dangerous lies.

The Living in Shadow and Light Truths we need to hold are:

For the women like me:

- Yes, people are as fabulous, good and amazing as you see them, feel them, believe them to be - but you need to listen, hear, watch as they tell you what they believe - because they will treat you from their belief, not yours;
- You can't imagine why someone would want to hurt you, because you would not knowingly hurt anyone, or anything, else - but shift your perception a bit... you might just be their reason to lash out, and it could have nothing to do with you - listen and respect what they will need to do in order to fit you into their vision and belief about their life
- You must listen to your own inner guidance, even if it is out of whack; don't take an action to hurt or harm someone else, even if others are pressuring you to fight back; however - and this is vital - don't keep allowing them to take advantage of you; remove yourself from their harm; and come to a better solution to interrupt the pattern of damage so you are taking care of yourself, and your values, at the same time
- Give yourself a break, and take a look at the dynamics in your own life, your own root origin tendencies, combined with the unbalanced areas you have been trying to sustain;
- You can begin to build yourself a way to be able to ask - ask for what you need, for help. This is a tough one, and

I'd love to say I have some insight and tools to integrate this one - but honestly I'm still grappling with it. Let's learn together, and with those who care for us and can help us build this 'ask for help' safely into our world?

For those of you with women you care about who are like me:

- See, hear, listen, grasp and try to understand her perspective from her point of view; she's telling you how she needs to see people, and life; blend that with yours, don't force yours upon her
- Eliminate the debate about who hurts whom, how often, and the human nature aspect; it's about discovering how to see the world as she does, at the same time being able to discover her own version of a 'threat meter' by accurately gauging the predominant life decisions others are living under
- Honor her nature, and not force, chide or encourage her to go against that nature; discover, the two of you, other ways to get her safe, more aware of dangers, more able to take care of herself and navigate life while keeping her sense of life views
- Take care not to draw with broad strokes; she is still smart, capable, and can take care of herself in a lot of ways; but she has some areas that are out of balance where she might not be fully aware of it - again discover her unique balance, not hand her yours and expect her to take it
- She can't, and won't, ask for help. You can't force her to, nor can you force upon her your idea of what 'help' would be; but you can offer to help her discover how to get what she needs in a way that strengthens her and shows her there can be safety in asking for help...

We can explore how I, and your woman like me, can reach these healthier points

Shadow and Light Better Questions #6

"If she is smart, capable, strong and makes it look very much like she's got the world on a string - but she is vulnerable and missing important clues - how can I help her discover that - and ways to factor in more safety for her?"

"How do I really listen, see, hear, and grasp her views about people and life - the ones that are important to her and central to her, while still helping her discover comfortable ways to protect herself, care for herself better?"

Next Steps:

To listen to audio, watch a video, or sit in - as my guest - on my next web masterclass about how to find your own root tendencies and strengthen them, your own way of living life through the decisions you've made about others - as well as how to see the behavior of others you need to be aware of -

- On the web, go to http://fourrootorigins.com/roxanneroot
- On your smartphone, text ROOT to 12264551275, and an invitation link will be sent back to you immediately
- Or, simply scan the code below from your smartphone:

♦ To find out more about Roxanne's "Dickens-Meets-Stephen-King" mashup, and how it applies to the cycles of domestic violence, visit http://domesticviolencesurivors.org/mashup

The Crowning Point of the Puzzle:

"We All Have A PoP"

One of the other fascinating, frustrating, and complicating things about us amazing humans is in our muddlement and confusion about what goes on inside our head.   Inside our heart.   Inside our spirit.   Inside our mind.   We aren't even aware of the problem because no one taught us what goes on in our own mind, head, heart and spirit.   We never got the toolbox of how it works, how your mind does what it does. We were missing the handbook on how your thoughts appear, and when. What a feeling is, for you.

We hit the ground running when we are born. We soak up so much, so fast, from so many directions.   The amount of sensory input into our little brains, bodies, and awareness is phenomenal.

We learn that the things we are putting in our mouths are part of our bodies, later we'll call them fingers and toes, and sometimes it's pretty uncomfortable if we chew on them. We learn to spit out those things others put in our mouths that we don't like. What they put in our mouths that we do like, and keep, eventually comes out the other end all different.   We learn that we can control when and where and how it comes out the other end, and that is a good thing.

We learn that we can stand, and move our legs to walk, then run, dance. We learn these finger things are useful for grabbing things - other things to put in our mouth - or running them across the fur of the cat feels really nice. We learn that we can get really good at using these finger things. We learn it's not the best idea to put peanut butter on the cat. We learn it is a good idea to curl up for a nap in the sun with the dog.

We learn to form words and associate banana with sweet and soft and sensual and yummy to eat - after you get rid of the rubbery outside thing - and how to let others know about that. We learn to form words and associate liver with icky and yucky and mealy and horrible and strong and how to let others know about that.

We grow and tie our shoes and throw a baseball and knit and play with friends and do math and make music and paint pictures and hold our pencil to put words on a page.

We learn so much, so fast, and so fully.

But, what we don't really get to learn is how we work, what happens inside our little minds and brains and emotions and senses.

We don't learn that because no one around us has the information to pass on to us like they do how to tie our shoes, add 73 and 49, or explain we don't like liver but it's irrelevant because it's your parents house and under their roof you do as you are told and there are children starving in Africa.

We don't know that our emotional states of being are

normal and necessary, and understanding them, combined with what we learned in our Four Roots chapter, is powerfully potent in having the life you want, the happiness you want, the wholeness and peace of mind you want.

When each of my client/friends found themselves ready to lash out, and lashing out at me would be good; when the drummer-turned-insurance-fraudster found himself ready to lash out, and lashing out at me would be good; when my husband in his violence was ready to lash out, and lashing out at me would be good; when Maggie and SuzyQ's mates were ready to lash out, and lashing out at them would be good...

When a person finds themselves in an emotional place to lash out, and direct that 'out' - outrage, outburst, outpouring, outlashing - toward another person - it's a misuse and misunderstanding, a lack of awareness, of what is happening inside themselves. All of that anger, instead of being used for something ultimately positive and beneficial, is instead used for destruction and negativity. It's not the anger that is the problem, it's how the anger is utilized that is the problem.

In our hierarchy of emotions, and states of being, there is a scale. Before my between homes and semi starvation exploration, I believed that we need to move up this scale.

That the more negative and damage causing/destruction inspiring emotional and mental states of being are 'downers' so that what we want to do is work our way 'up.' Move from our down in the dumps slumps up into the neutral emotional and mental states of being, and then further up into the positive and restoration causing/healing inspiring emotional and mental states of being.

When I began to rebuild, to start teaching and sharing this work anew, I needed to take myself as a client first. Discovering those wrinkles, those hiccups and the depths of my own lost and self defeating, self destructive, life decisions, to begin my own healing I needed to put to use my own strategies, tools and systems.

I began using the fresh insight and deeper meaning discovered during these desolate times. In fleshing out the hierarchy of emotional and mental states of being, I was whipping through the downer states, explaining them and detailing them with ease.

Despair. Depression. Powerlessness. Lost. Desperate. Hurt. Heartbreak. Aloneness. Loneliness. Betrayal. Anger. Blame. Retribution. Frustration. Humiliation. Shame.

Yup, got those. Entire volumes about what they are, particularly how they show up and express themselves in each of the four root types, and then the auditory, kinesthetic or visual engagement comforts. How they each show up in feeling, in thought, and in emotion - all different states of being. What they mean when they show up in each of those forms, for you, us, as individuals.

Powerful, powerful stuff.

Got my way into the neutral zone: Indifference. Neutrality. Complacency. Their similar states. Cool, nifty, good, whipped through those.

Now we find ourselves in the 'good stuff' end of the spectrum. Happy. Joyful. Excited. Hopeful. Blissful. Peaceful. Contented. Fulfilled. Eager.

And, nothing. My describing my own emotional states ground to a resounding and obvious halt. I couldn't describe any happy, good, or joyful moment outside of one having directly to do with my happy marriage before the death of my husband, or with direct interaction with an animal. For me, just on my own, in my world and my life, I could not describe what happy was. None of the beneficial and good mental/emotional states of being.

It drew me up short, and I threw myself more fully into these theories, into results I'd achieved with others.

It was then I realized I had been working backwards.

What we want is to know ourselves, to be conscious of our own life, to be self aware and self determining.

What we have seems as if we are **subject to** our thoughts, our feelings, our emotions, and our mental states. We are spending our days reacting to how we feel feeling, express an emotion or a thought we think. We have trouble telling the difference between a thought and a feeling and an emotion. They are so intertwined in our awareness...is it the chicken and egg thing? Which comes first - the emotion, feeling or thought? Aren't they all the same experience, just using a different word to explain that?

We don't believe that they are in our ability to understand, and to use for our own benefit (I don't like the concept of 'control' because it is widely used in the sense of restricting, of diminishing and of denial, rather than of interaction).

We are disconnected from our own minds and emotions and feelings and they way we work. The way they work in our lives. The way we should work with them instead of denying them or allowing them to fling us around in constant reaction to them.

So the downer and negative state is really one of the greatest disconnects with the person we really are, our roots, our wholeness. Powerlessness, anger, despair and depression are the farthest away from the full connection with our whole selves. These states of being are far on the edge, away from the strong, aware, balanced being that is healthy. The healthiest mental, emotionally, spiritually (not religionistically, but that essence or spirit of you).

What we want is to work our way in, away from those negative states of being, in toward our wholeness and health... even if you are an outward expression tendency type...you want to feel, to know, to be, whole and healthy in your own life.

When we are whole, healthy and connected, aware and conscious of our own inner workings - mind, thoughts, brain, feeling, emotion - then we have the power to make choices and decisions based on that all powerful self knowledge and awareness.

Once we understand, see clearly, and know that our emotions and feelings and thoughts no longer control us, we no longer react to them, they no longer seem random and unpredictable.

Quite the opposite, we now know.

The power in our own life and world comes from:

✓ Understanding our state of emotional being at any given time
✓ how it fits with us and because of us as individuals - your state for you, mine for me, every individual for themselves
✓ Where that state of being, at that moment, relative to what is going on with you at the time, fits on your state of being scale

In the case of domestic violence, both the deliverer and receiver are in extreme disconnect from their own awareness and power in their own emotional and mental state of being, not acknowledging and respecting their own feelings. Perhaps not in all phases and areas of their lives, but definitely in those areas contributing to this destructive relationship. We have different states of being in each area.

- o We might choose words such as comfortable, capable, strong, self reliant and happy in our line work, the work we perform and carry out ourselves.
- o We might choose words such as uneasy, off balance, insecure, worried, stressed to describe the way we are in the company we work for.
- o We have relative states of being for all parts of our life - love, parents, family, talents, skills, work, kids, hobbies, mates, ex mates, money, home, etc.
- o We can have different states of being, all over the map, relating to each of these different life aspects.

In the case of domestic violence, outbursts come out of the realm of powerlessness, of feeling trapped, of pain and utmost discomfort. When a naturally outward expressing root origin type is in those states of being, simply experiencing these states, the next natural step is anger. When a naturally inward expressing root origin type is in those states of being, simply experiencing these states, the next step is to quiet them.

Outward expression of anger needs blame. It needs to be assigned to someone, something, else. It takes self balance, takes stability, to accept personal responsibility for ones own state of being, of feeling, of what is happening. This requires the state of stability to be okay with self examination and self discovery. You need to be pretty firmly in happy and peaceful - or even entrenched in a neutral state of being - in order to examine a part of yourself that might not be pretty or comfortable. In order to examine your life or yourself, at all.

When you are in the negative states of powerless and hurting and all of that energy builds up into anger, you are in no position for self evaluation and exploration as to your contribution to your own powerlessness. Not gonna happen.

But you need the anger, we all do. We all need anger as a healthy part of life. Anger is good and beneficial. Anger is rocket fuel to blast out of the pain and the powerlessness. You need something huge, something explosive, to push you out of the gravitational pull that pain and powerlessness have.

Blame helps. Here, at this point, it's necessary and it's a good thing. It's their fault. It's them, they did this to you! It's not your fault. Get good and cranked and angry and blameful and spiteful and full of piss and vinegar at the whole situation and at them.

It's her fault. It's her fault you are hurting, or ashamed, or embarrassed or humiliated or uncomfortable. It's your child's fault. Blame them, get good and angry. It's your bosses fault, your governments fault, your parents fault, your best friends fault.

But, had this fault, anger and blame with awareness and understanding that this is natural, and it's what you need to do where you are. Kind of like in the middle of childbirth when the woman you love and adore finds you all kinds of bad and evil.   This is your fault, and it's not good.   But it's a consequence of the moments at hand.

Moments which are designed to pass.

Anger, blame, retribution, are not to be acted on against someone else, or yourself. Now is not the time to wrap those thoughts of words, of fists, of calling friends and strangers to spew, of picking up the gun, the axe, the knife. It's not time to take the feeling of needing to spew, explode, make them pay for what they have done. It's not time to get retribution for the hurt, the fear, the powerless.

They are to show you that something very important is happening with you which is making you feel like you are not in control of your own life and what happens in it. That you are focusing your attention on something that you believe is wrong, and should be different, but you can't make it different. And that is seventeen thousand forms of unacceptable. You know that it is natural and right to be the chooser and decider and determiner of how you feel and what happens in your life. To be in any way other than that is simply not acceptable.

The size and scope of the blame, the anger, the hurt, the retribution, the reaction is equal to the size and scope of your feeling of powerlessness and 'it's not right' and "I'm going to do something about this, rightthisminute."

It's exactly proportional so that it, the anger, the blame, the retribution, the vitriol, is enough to propel you directly out of your powerless and disconnect, and closer to being able to take action and regain your own power. Where, in thinking smarter, feeling stronger, being more emotionally balanced, you can come up with more appropriate, beneficial, solution oriented ways to deal with this thing that is so important to you.

You need a helluva movement to get you from powerless and mad as hell about it into productively in your own power. They are opposite states of being, of living, of interacting.

One is likely more comfortable, more present, more prevalent, and stronger - and that one is likely the powerlessness one. We humans practice our painful, angry, hurt and hurtful negative feelings, emotions, thoughts and state more often.

Because you haven't practiced, gotten to know, lived, been aware of, heard and clearly seen the scope of your own power, your own happy, your own steady and balanced - it is going to be quite the thing to get you there. It's like realizing you've been in an igloo all your life but what would make things perfect is a tropical beach. You can describe the beach, get a good sense of it, have a good understanding of it - but because you've never really lived in the sand with the sun on your skin, it's going to take a new life skill set to make that your way of living.

Anger, blame, self justification is designed to be something strong enough to get you out of down and powerless. To get you out of the igloo and laying on that beach in the sun.

It is absolutely not designed for you to take action. Any action taken in anger and blame harms you, as the action taker, as well as the intended receiver. Nothing beneficial comes of it. You can blame the snow, the ice, the igloo and the cold - but it won't change one thing to get you to the beach.

To understand the power and place of your anger is to be able to use it to solve your real internal problem. To give yourself a heads up that important stuff is going on here. Icy igloo: bad; warm toasty beach: good.

To take your own life and get out of your powerlessness and pain, and to stay there. You choose warm, sun, waves, sand. It's exclusively in your power to have that preferred state of being.

Only you can do that. You cannot depend upon, rely upon or even expect someone else to change their behavior so that you feel powerful and in control of your own life. The igloo and ice are not going to be able to be forced, berated or connived into becoming sand and sun.

In fact, it isn't them, it's you. Your interaction with them, her, it, is only serving to show you that you feel powerless and you need to get your own power back. To see where you lost your power, where you feed your hurt, so you can then heal, solve, remove it.

It's an inside job, your powerless and disconnect.

It's an inside job, your power and control over your own life.

When the inward expressing root origin types are in powerless, since their natural movement is action in, not out, they hurt themselves.

They blame, but blame themselves. They get upset and angry, but with themselves. Even if they include anger and blame at someone else, they take fuller personal self responsibility for the problem.

The rocket fuel to propel them out into more power and happier is much harder to find with this root type. It's how they forgive, it's how they take the blame, it's how they understand how someone could be angry or mean or hurtful toward them - it is our fault.

Getting to our happy healthy and taking self responsibility for our blame and self destruction is a different path. Our anger isn't rocket fuel out, it is tempered and dampened and unacceptable. We don't get angry and lash out. We don't hurt other people. We might get good and angry, but because we are in no way comfortable acting on it, we actually make our own problems worse. We turn more powerfully in on ourselves in reaction.

We need to understand our blame, our making excuses for

others bad behavior, and that bad behavior directed toward us, is part of our disconnect. Our healthy, connected state of being knows we aren't to blame for everything. We can retain our compassion and our nurture, but we can find that place of taking responsibility for our own protection of feelings and body at the same time.

That is very opposite for us. The opposite state of being for the outward expressing type to understand the vast difference between feeling angry/powerless/blame and feeling in control/powerful/self responsible. The opposite state of being for us inward expressing type is to feel self reliant/self accepting/self forgiving.

Understanding your natural root engagement tendency, combining that with the hierarchy of our mental/emotional/thinking states of being, allow each of us to take self control and self responsibility for our own thoughts, our own feelings, our own emotions, and our own actions.

It's the most powerful aspect of the strategy and system to understand and interrupt domestic violence communication issues. It's the missing piece in our human self understanding and relationship successes.

It breaks down into a simple formula I call "The PoPSystem":

Your current Place of Perception - where you are now, how it feels, how you see it, what it seems like

Your Place of Preference - where you would prefer to be, how you would rather feel, how you want to see it, what you want it to be like

Then, knowing those points - your now and what you want that is different, combine that with how the mental and emotional hierarchy and steps work - you plot your individual

Path of Progress - step by conscious, aware, powerful step to get you from where you are now to where you want to be

You will always know when you are disconnected, how, and its effect on your thoughts, emotions and feelings, so you can determine your actions before its too late. You will always know how to reconnect, the distance between your now and where you want to be, and how to get there.

No longer will you be engaging in violent outbursts, hurting others, blaming others for your own thoughts and feelings. No longer will you be engaging in receiving violent outbursts, feeling responsible for others thoughts and feelings.

For the woman you love who is being abused, you will be able to clearly see where she is in her disconnect and help her walk her way to her own personal strength; and for the man you care about who is being abusive, you can understand how and why this is happening, helping him restore his own power and understand his anger.

Next Steps

To discover more about your hierarchy of states of being,

how these thoughts, feelings and emotions show up in your life, and in the lives of the men and women you care about with domestic violence, sit in on my latest masterclass as my gift,

- ◆ On the web, visit http://thepopsystem.com/lisal;
- ◆ On your smartphone, text POPSYSLIS to 12264551275 and a way to access the audio and masterclass will be sent to you
- ◆ Or, simply scan the code below from your smartphone:

Shadow and Light Lie #7
"Gender, Gay, Bi, Inter-racial, Etc, Bias!"

Throughout this book I've used the traditional male/female in the examples.

Please, do not for a moment, regard that as anything other than example.

I'd prefer if instead of looking at gender you could see the root engagement, the tendencies in a person, and their easiest life engagement modalities.

This, relationship, relationships out of whack, this is life stuff. It lives in our emotions, in our thoughts, in our beliefs, in what we tell ourselves. It lives in our views, our choices and our decisions. It lives on the inside, not the outside, this life stuff.

Life stuff happens to humans. Tall ones, short ones. Old ones, young ones. Purple ones, pink ones, green ones, cream ones and brown ones. Humans with male kind of genitalia, and with female kind of genitalia.

Humans with all manner of quirks, of eccentricities. Godknows I have more than my fair share of eccentricities.

Love, living, life, heart and soul are human conditions. They are all we have to work with.

You, no matter if you are in one of the descriptions above, or not, are a unique, one of a kind, amazing individual.

I don't really care if you don't know that, or if you don't believe that. If not, someone has sold you a load of crap otherwise. Let it go, and discover your value for yourself, on your own terms.

So, this book, this work, these conversations are about people. Humans.

Identify with the roots, the underlying energies, patterns and human aspects. I did not intend to make it gender specific or gender delineated.

I chose the examples based on two criteria:

They were good examples of a common and easily recognized root tendency and imbalance;
And, the people involved were easily reachable, agreeing when I asked if I could mold their journeys resoundingly in the light - if I made sure that no one but a small handful of confidants would be able to place them in the story.

That's it. The whole agenda.

We can explore how, no matter the gender or other factors, you can reach this healthier point

Shadow and Light Better Questions #7

"If this isn't about race, economic status, gender, age, and all the other comfortable excuses I've held to keep this issue out of my life, how can I be more aware of the real issues with domestic violence?"

"If I stop using my race, gender, age, socioeconomic class, gay, bi, transgender, or other life engagement type as my excuse to overlook domestic violence, what do I do then?"

Next Steps:

To listen to audio, watch a video, or sit in - as my guest - on my next web masterclass about how to let go of the domestic violence stereotypes so we can all be part of the solution -

- On the web, go to http:// domesticviolencesolutionsalliance.org/nostereotype
- On your smartphone, text STEREOTYPE to 12264551275, and an invitation link will be sent back to you immediately
- Or, simply scan the code below from your smartphone:

What Now?

"Punish the Fruit for Being Sour and it Will Return to Sweet"

The Biggest Lie of All

We need, as people, neighborhoods, societies - as you, and me, and the men & women we love - to take an overview understanding of that outside role in domestic violence. In any type of violence we perpetrate on one another.

We've taken a look at some basic life root engagement tendencies. Those are vital to understanding the 'why we do what we do' as humans.

Starting with, focusing on, the root 'why' in all behavior provides us a freedom to discover what causes the behavior. Until we know, see, grasp and understand what causes behavior, we can never change that behavior.

I love the simpler analogy of a plant and its fruit. We see that the fruit, where we are expecting sweet and juicy, is stringy and sour, instead. We can berate, punish, lash out at, unleash our anger and rage on that stringy fruit until we drop from exhaustion.

We can hand down edicts, sign court orders, enact stringent laws, assign police guards, even isolate this fruit from other fruit on its tree.

The problem is, we take all these actions with the honest belief that this fruit will some how wake up, wise up, and get sweet and juicy, pronto! Fruit - change, now. Done.

Because, we shared our righteous anger and indignation, we demanded, we attempted force, we asserted our authority on this fruit. Clearly, this stringy sour thing will now straighten up, fly right (so to speak, fruit-wise) and get with the program.

What does this fruit think it is? We have been good citizens to stand out and stand up against this stringy, sour, fruit. We can pat ourselves on the back for throwing all of our attention and might at this stringy sour situation.

You know what?

It's still a stringy sour fruit.

Because it doesn't know how to be different. It isn't even really sure there is something wrong, because it its little fruit life, it's always been stringy and sour. As far back as it can recall, in its little fruit memory, it's just been what it is. Stringy. And sour.

We probably aren't the first to deride the little fruit for it, either. It probably caught it from the other fruit on the tree long before we arrived to notice. Maybe it began life nice and juicy and sweet, but some outside factor interrupted its root nutrients, and the best it can do, now, is be sour and stringy to stay alive.

We keep pushing, and it's getting defensive, because it's doing the best it can, and we are making it feel worthless, wrong and punished.

We lose. The sour fruit loses. The whole tree loses.

That is what we do, as a society, as people, when a person is out of balance and displays behavior which reflects, demonstrates, that out of balance.

Healthy, happy, well balanced people are not the ones climbing the clock tower with granddad's semi automatic rifle to pick off their local townsfolk.

Healthy, happy, well balanced people don't beat, berate, rape, torture, harm, denigrate, steal from, slander, threaten or murder their mate, their kids, friends and other people.

Isn't there a basic simplicity in that?

So when we see this behavior, clearly, something is amiss in the person taking the detrimental action.

This person is equivalent to the sour stringy fruit.

If this person knew how to behave differently, healthier, more beneficial - they would. Somehow we got this weird notion that people deliberately, clearly, and knowingly, make horrible decisions and choices.

As if this person wakes up in the morning, stretches in bed, greets the day, and their thoughts are akin to "You know what? Today I'm going to choose the most destructive and worst decisions, choices and actions I possibly can! That's the ticket!"

The truth is, no matter how bad, how dangerous, how disconnected and evil a behavior looks - to the person engaging in the behavior it is the best they - in their world, in their mind, in their choices - can do.

Not your world. Not your decisions. Not your choices and how you would, or would not make them.

In the singular world of the individual carrying out the

behavior.

Even if they did wake up and say those words, it would be because they actually believe those words are the best they can do. Even in the worst of bad choices and decisions I made, I was still doing the best I can with what I thought - what I believed - I had to work with.

When you begin with the premise, belief, that you are worthless garbage, ineffective at taking even the most simple care of yourself, where do you go from there, decision/action - wise?

Because something is amiss. Something below the surface, underneath the behavior and action, is amiss.

We, as societies and people, treat them as the sour stringy fruit. We look only at the outside appearance, the behavior, the result.

As the sour stringy fruit, we fully expect this lost, damaged, individual to see the error of his or her ways, and fix themselves. Poof. Like magic.

Going back to our fruit -

In order to change the sour stringy fruit into its natural, intended, state of sweet and juicy, we need to be curious about why this fruit turned out so different. We need to think about restoring, not destroying. The change is an encouragement of health, not a destruction of what is amiss. What is going on resulting in a sweet juicy fruit turning stringy and sour?

The underlying 'why' is the only thing that matters.

A bit of investigation will likely determine what is impacting the life of this fruit so harmfully. By determining what is the root cause of the sour stringy, we know what to adjust, where to tweak, how to fix.

By giving the fruit what it needs to be sweet, and juicy, and healthy...the fruit can go about becoming healthier, sweeter and juicier. We can restore the internal balance, and the sweet juicy takes care of itself. The fruit must reflect the root - it can be no other way.

Helping solve the underlying problem effects real change. It's a waste of time berating the fruit for lacking what it needs to be healthy, as is demanding the fruit be healthy.

You can't heal the root by manipulating the fruit. You just get more rotten fruit. Heal the root, heal the fruit.

You can't repair the damaged person by demanding they be different. You just get a more damaged person. You can't repair a damaged person by punishing them into healthy self balance. You just get a deeper imbalanced person.

Isn't it time for better questions? Better answers? Better solutions? Actually discovering solutions? Growing out of our perpetual anger and moving into a powerful force for changing and removing the problems at their source?

I believe so.

Don't you?

Next Steps:

To listen to audio, watch a video, or sit in - as my guest - on my next web masterclass about how to learn to find where the imbalance begins in the real root of a situation, person, event -

so we can begin restoring balance - visit

- ◆ On the web, go to http://fourrootorigins.com/fruit
- ◆ On your smartphone, text FRUIT to 12264551275, and an invitation link will be sent back to you immediately
- ◆ Or, simply scan the code below from your smartphone

Shadow and Light Lie #8
"I Don't Know What To Do But There Must Be An Easy Answer"
And
"There Must Be An Easy Way To Fix This"

Solutions to the domestic violence issues, once we are aware we need them - and the systems we are now using are broken - aren't easy.

And, they are easy.

I know that seems contradictory and in a way it is.

As we briefly shone the light throughout this book on a few examples of abuse, there are as many examples of domestic violence, spousal abuse and destructive behavior as there are people involved in the relationships.

If we start with something as basic as a normal, run of the mill, every day couple (and let's pretend for the moment that such a couple exists...):

- There are two individuals interacting with each other
- There are misunderstandings, hurt feelings, expectations, harmonies, disagreements
- There are commitments, promises, irritations, laughter, pressures, growth

And no two relationships are alike.

Similarities, yes.

When we add in the dynamics of an abusive relationship, those

imbalances, the damages;
Add in the outside factors like family, law, community;
Plus other internal factors like health, children, finances…

We have a collection of highly unique, highly individualized,
    exceptionally one of a kind
dynamics.

The solutions are as unique, individualized, and one of a kind
    as the relationship.

I've intended this book to start the conversation, to break open
some stagnant and long held beliefs. I've wanted to give some
new food for thought, some better questions…

There is no way, no matter how much I want to be able to, that
I can - or anyone can - provide a nifty lightweight one size fits
all formula for resolving.

But, I can open the window so we stop banging our faces
against the glass.

Throughout the book I've ended each chapter with an
invitation to take a step. Take a step for more. Take a step into
your questions. Take a step to discover your answers. Take a
step toward that individualized, highly unique, custom fit
solution.

That is all we can do. Ask more, discover more. Put the puzzle
pieces together that match the individual and unique
relationships.

We've got a fully loaded tool chest, a kitchen full of ingredients.
Now it's up to us to step away from this book and its fixed
pages to start building and cooking up a storm of solutions.

I invite you, again, to take those steps - for you and for the woman you love, the man you love, the family you love.

Because, we aren't talking about solutions for anger, domestic violence, spousal abuse, abuser, victim, child, family....

The solutions can't be found in the anger, in the violence, in the abuse, in the abuser or the victim and child...

We are talking about healing a human being from the inside out. We are talking about balancing minds, clearing thoughts, mending broken spirits and souls.

Balance the mind, clear the thinking, mend the broken heart, spirit, soul, heal the human - and the violence can no longer 'be.'

It's healing the root, and the fruit will sweeten and come to life.

Shadow and Light Better Questions - Now & Future

"This has opened me up to thinking about it, seeing it a different way, and I feel I want to know more....how do I discover solutions?"

Next Steps:

To listen to audio, watch a video, or sit in - as my guest - on my next web masterclass about how to find out about the solutions we can, together, create and bring to life - please

◆ On the web, go to http://

domesticviolencesolutionsalliance.org/lisal

◆ On your smartphone, text ALLIANCE to 12264551275, and an invitation link will be sent back to you immediately

◆ Or, simply scan the code below from your smartphone:

About the Author

Roxanne Whatley is the founder of the "Domestic Violence Solutions Alliance. Org" (http://domesticviolencesolutionsalliance.org/lisal), where they actively engage in more powerful training and classes to break the dangerous cycles of abuse. The organization works in all areas of domestic violence:

- providing insight and training for professionals and first responders, law enforcement in domestic violence cases;
- for shelter and rescue groups dealing with victims;
- for professional counselors serving the domestic violence cycle - both abuser and victim.

They conduct outreach, education and integration of materials to stop the cycles of abuse for for the workplace, schools, with kids, women, mens groups as well as those areas of incarceration for those involved in domestic violence.

She is also the founder of "Domestic Violence Survivors. Org" (http://domesticviolencesurvivors.org/lisal) where she devotes her time to helping those who have been on the receiving end of domestic violence replace the symptoms of being a victim to the more supportive life skills of being a survivor. Often when relating personal stories of the events of domestic abuse the label of 'victim' is assigned, sometimes in a derogatory manner. It's important to come together to know that it doesn't matter how outsiders view you, it matters that you know you are no longer a victim, but a survivor. As survivors we can be of the best example to others trying to pull themselves out of the clutches of abusive relationships. We can also be a powerful voice in society to help others understand how to interrupt domestic violence at its source.

Roxanne was the first recipient and inspiration for the "Hathor" award (http://hathorawards.com/lisal), given for leadership and excellence in supporting women in crisis from domestic violence and abuse, and fostering a more potent dialog about the issues we face regarding battered woman syndrome. Through her production company, Vanadis Films (http://vanadisfilms.com/lisal) she is producing the documentary "Living In Shadow and Light" (http://livinginshadowandlightmove.com/lisal) about the issues we face surrounding domestic violence, and how to provide better solutions to save the women we love.

Through the Institute for Healing Hearts and Minds (http://instituteforhealingheartandmind.org/lbm), Roxanne provides tools, training and masterclasses for improving all areas of intimate relationships. Two of her most popular trainings are based on her soon to be published books: "UnBreak Your Marriage" (http:// unbreakyourmarriagebook.com/lisal) for those couples caught in a troubled marriage and how to rediscover their healthy love; and, "Stop Dating, Start SoulMating" (http://stopdatingstartsoulmatingbook.com/ lisal)for men and women who are ready to find - and live - the love relationship they really want.

When not safely tucked in her shadows, Roxanne has just come out in the light to play and can sometimes be found on twitter: @RoxanneWhatley; Instagram: theRoxanneWhatley; and FaceBook: http://facebook.com/iamRoxanneWhatley

She lives in the country with her deaf cat, her horse (both rescues), a couple of elderly sheep, a one horned steer, and various other wildlife. You can find out more about Roxanne and her work through her website RoxanneWhatley.com

On your smartphone, go to Roxanne's site as a starting point by scanning this QR code: